A CENTURY OF SAIL

A CENTURY OF SAIL

Invergordon Boating Club 1901-2001

BY

JOHN McMILLAN

ISBN 0-9541023-0-4

The Club is grateful for the gift of support towards this publication from:

Bannermans of Tain
Caley Marina
Bilgewater Gin

Typeset in Times Roman 12pt.

Published by The Invergordon Boating Club

Printed by Gospel Truth Press, Invergordon

Contents

Foreword

By Alan Whiteford
Chairman of Cromarty Firth Port Authority.

In chronicling the history of the Invergordon Boating Club, John McMillan has created an important document about life on the waters of the Cromarty Firth. Running in parallel with the momentous naval and oil industry periods for this famous harbour, the Boating Club has been sustained by the enthusiasm of its membership and has happily co-existed with, and adapted to, other users.

From inception by its founding fathers in 1901 the club, like the firth itself, has experienced fluctuating fortunes but has stood the test of time. This book tells the story of the Boating Club's voyage through the 20th century, introduces us to the characters who have contributed to its history and explains, often in a humourous way, how important the club has been to its own community.

The author's love for his subject is evident throughout the book and his affection for fellow club members both past and present is obvious. It is a story that needed to be told and John McMillan tells it in his own inimitable way. Many people who care for the club and the Cromarty Firth will undoubtedly share in his enjoyment.

Alan Whiteford,

May 2001.

Acknowledgement

I am indebted to Jean Cheyne, Ron Stewart, Denis Slattery and Liz Fraser who have done most of the groundwork for this book. They gathered information from members past and present and others in the community with memories of the club and Jean steered the book through the publication process. Many members of the community willingly gave of their time to be interviewed. There are too many to list all the names here but they may have the satisfaction of knowing that their cherished memories, as well as their hospitality, have been valued. It has not been possible to include all their stories in such a small book. I hope they can forgive any omissions. Present members too have been generous with their time and courageously frank with their admissions. These are the people who have breathed life into the story of Invergordon Boating Club. Eileen MacAskill of Inverness, Bob Steward the Highland Council Archivist and the staff of Highland Council Libraries at Invergordon, Dingwall, Inverness and Lochcarron have helped locate relevant information and useful background reading. Their assistance has been much appreciated as has that of The Scottish Maritime Museum at Irvine, The National Maritime Museum, Greenwich, The Royal Naval Museum, Portsmouth, The British Museum, Inverness Museum and the Archives and Business Centre of Glasgow University. Thanks are also due to a host of local people, Kathy Mansfield, marine photographer and writer, and Beken of Cowes for their permission to print photographs.

The minute books and other records of Invergordon Boating Club have been the primary source of information supplemented by reports from The Inverness Courier, The Inverness Advertiser and Ross-shire Chronicle, The Invergordon Times, The Ross-shire Journal, The Press and Journal, The Herald (formerly The Glasgow Herald) and The Times. Many other books and magazines have been consulted but the excellent book This Noble Harbour by Marinell Ash must be recommended for those interested in finding out more about the development of the Cromarty Firth.

Every effort has been made to check the accuracy of information but in such a task it is possible when transcribing notes for errors to occur. If these exist, the errors are mine. Finally, I must acknowledge the valuable help, tolerance and unfailing patience of Mr John Munro of The Gospel Truth Press at the printing stage. He postponed a well earned retirement to see this project through.

John B McMillan,
Lochcarron.

May 2001.

Chapter One

Setting the Scene

In spite of its deep water and good shelter, the Cromarty Firth has remained relatively undeveloped for commercial and recreational activity until recent times. Although favoured by mariners for many centuries as a temporary anchorage, its narrow entrance with a strong tidal stream presented problems in the days when ships relied only on the wind for propulsion. Daniel Defoe, the author of Robinson Crusoe, had been considerably impressed by the potential of the Cromarty Firth as a safe anchorage for the Royal Navy of Great Britain. He had been sent to Scotland in 1706 to prepare a report for the Prime Minister of England prior to the impending Union of the Parliaments. His report indicated that there was relatively little commercial shipping in these parts at the time and concluded: *'this noble harbour is left entirely useless in the world'.* It was a harbour whose time was yet to come.

By the end of the 18th century the town of Cromarty at the entrance to the firth had established itself as an industrial, fishing and commercial centre and a seaport of some significance; it was also a stopping point for vessels bound for North America. By contrast, Invergordon at that time had been described by one observer as *'an ugly village in an important situation'*; but its potential was recognised by MacLeod of Cadboll in 1828 when he built the harbour with two piers, one straight, the other L shaped. His vision and enterprise were rewarded. Invergordon, with better road links to the rest of the country, now overtook Cromarty as the centre of marine activity in the Cromarty Firth and soon had established regular steamship links with Inverness, Aberdeen, Leith, the west coast and even fortnightly sailings to London. Whisky and grain were exported; imports included timber, tiles, coal, salt, books, drapery, clothes and musical instruments. Fashionable ladies' hats from London and Paris could now be obtained from the shops in Invergordon High Street.

Until 200 years ago the word yacht was used to describe a fast sailing vessel designed for the transportation of royalty and other dignitaries of state. The word is an anglicisation of the Dutch word *jacht* derived from the word for hunt, hence a yacht was a boat capable of fast movement. Prior to the development of road and rail networks in the 19th century, transportation by sea was relatively fast and reliable. Inevitably, owning a yacht became fashionable among the aristocracy, but more for social activity rather than racing. The Cork Water Club, formed in 1720 and now called Cork Royal Yacht Club, is the oldest yachting club in the British Isles. The first recorded race was on the Thames from Greenwich to the Nore and back in 1749. In the 19th century yachtsmen began to influence naval architecture when the Earl of Belfast built the beautiful *Waterwitch* and in 1851 wagered 1000 guineas that he could outsail any naval vessel. He would cruise to and fro outside Portsmouth harbour waiting for naval ships to come out and then shame the navy by consistently outsailing them. As a result, the naval architects began to reconsider ship design in order to produce faster vessels.

With sail beginning to give way to steam propulsion in the middle of the 19th century, easier access brought several wealthy visitors to the Cromarty Firth in steam yachts, exploration of the Scottish Highlands and Islands having become a fashionable activity among an aristocracy intrigued by a region virtually unknown to most who lived beyond its boundaries.

One of the early yachting explorers was Prince Napoleon, the nephew of Napoleon Bonaparte. Having commanded the 3rd French division in the Crimean War which ended in April 1856, he embarked on what was described in the Inverness Advertiser as a scientific cruise to Scotland and Iceland in June. Leaving his ship at Peterhead, he travelled over three hundred miles through the Highlands visiting Aberdeen, Deeside, Braemar and Blair Athol, then north to Inverness. After a brief stay at the Caledonian Hotel, he re-joined his magnificent yacht at Cromarty, driving straight through the town in his carriage to the harbour. The Invergordon Times reported on 2 July that his lack of interest in stopping to savour the attractions of Cromarty apparently caused offence to some of its citizens who thought so highly of it. His ship immediately left for Thurso where, having some letters to despatch, he did grace that town with a visit the following day.

A portly figure bearing a remarkable resemblance to his more famous uncle, his enjoyment of his trip was expressed in a letter written by one of his aides, part of which appeared in the Inverness Courier: *'He is all activity and makes those about him as much alive as himself. It is impossible to imagine a more agreeable voyage and the only illness was when three of our party became rather qualmish for an hour or so in a rough sea.'* This probably refers to that part of the voyage through the turbulent waters of the Pentland Firth.

He was later followed by many others. As the British Empire reached its zenith towards the end of the 19th century, the enormous industrial output of the country and its dominant position in world trade had generated considerable wealth, albeit for a relatively small section of the population. Interest in yachting had been growing steadily since the start of the century and many of those who had amassed large fortunes could afford to lavish vast sums of money on luxurious vessels and pay for crews to man them. But racing in sleek boats was exciting the interest of a wider public. Yacht building in Scotland had started on the Clyde in 1803 and by the middle of the century the public enjoyed the spectacle of graceful yachts racing in the sheltered waters of the Clyde and the Forth.

During the Victorian era the British population at large had developed a love affair with the seaside in the common belief that fresh sea air was good for health. Coastal holiday resorts were now booming, an extensive rail network making them accessible to a working-class population which could escape, if only for a day's outing, from the grime-laden air of the industrial centres. A culture of recreation had developed, encouraged by a national concern for the health of the population; the era of organised sport had begun with the formal establishment of associations to promote competition in Cricket, Football and Rugby and, with a proliferation of yacht clubs around the country, the Royal Yachting Association was formed in 1876. Yacht racing had already become an international sport in 1851 when an American yacht, the *America,* sailed across the Atlantic to win the Round the Island Race at Cowes. The cup it won was later offered for competition in 1870 and became known as the America's Cup, gaining the status of the 'premier yacht race in the world.'

In a maritime nation with the largest empire in world history and with thousands of men employed in world-wide shipping trade, the newspapers of the time carried many columns of shipping news. By the middle of the century unofficial ocean racing was taking place annually as those thoroughbreds of the British Mercantile Service, the tea clippers, raced home with each new season's cargo of tea from China, the first boat home always securing the top price for its cargo. With elegant yacht-like hulls, these were the fastest and most beautiful sailing ships yet to grace the world's oceans and they captured the attention of the nation like no others have ever done.

Probably no ocean race ever excited so much interest as The Great Tea Race of 1866 for which the tea merchants offered an extra 10 shillings per ton of tea and a prize of £100 to the captain of the first ship home. Huge sums of money were wagered by owners, crews and shipping agents; even in land-locked sleepy villages people daily scanned the shipping columns of the newspapers for news of the racing clippers. In the shipping community the event matched the excitement of the Derby or the Boat Race when, in May 1866, sixteen of the finest clippers assembled at anchor off Foochow to wait for the tea coming down the river. Three ships, *Ariel, Taeping* and *Serica,* all Clyde-built with Scottish captains, slipped their moorings on the same tide at Foochow on the evening of 28th May; ninety nine days and twelve thousand miles later the same three ships arrived off Dungeness to pick up pilots with *Ariel* a mere five minutes ahead of *Taeping* and *Serica* only four hours behind. The three ships also docked at the Thames on the same tide. *Taeping* entered London Docks 20 minutes ahead of *Ariel* which, with a greater draught, was delayed by the tide before entering the East India Docks. *Serica* docked only 90 minutes later. So close was the finish it was decided to share the prizes between *Ariel* and *Taeping*. The newspapers published sensational accounts of this astonishing race and The Inverness Advertiser and Ross-shire Chronicle described the race as *'a remarkable instance of the skill and exactitude of modern navigation ... and an unparalleled feat considering the passage lasted more than three months.'*

Prints of a famous painting of *Ariel* and *Taeping* racing side by side in this great event are still to be found hanging on the walls of many homes throughout the country.

In the next two decades however, even their remarkable achievements were eclipsed by two new ships which were to become icons in the sailing world, *Cutty Sark* and *Thermopylae*. The British public had developed an interest in fast sailing ships.

Local public interest was also greatly aroused by the increasing use of the Cromarty Firth by the ships of the Royal Navy as a short term anchorage; the extension of the railway system north of Inverness in 1863 had opened up better transport links so that fuel, provisions and personnel could now be moved more easily. By the early years of the 20th century, Invergordon was established as a fuelling and repair base for the Royal Navy and the huge fleets of ships of the world's largest and most powerful navy became a common sight in its waters with enormous benefit to the local economy.

By the turn of the century a widespread fascination for ships had developed; wherever large numbers of warships, merchantmen, fishing boats or pleasure craft assembled, they aroused the interest of spectators. Sailing had become a popular pastime among the landowning, business and professional classes. Racing and cruising were now commonplace in British inshore waters and, on the east coast, the Cromarty Firth provided the best sheltered water for recreational sailing between the Tay and the Orkneys as well as the spectacle of large warships and beautiful steam yachts. A club at Cromarty had already been started and a growing number of small boats were sailing in the waters off Invergordon. The time had come for Invergordon Boating Club to be born. Its character in its formative years was determined by these various influences.

Chapter Two

The Early Years 1901-1914

On 3rd July 1901, a group of gentlemen interested in the formation of a boating club met in the North of Scotland Bank at Invergordon, now the Clydesdale Bank. This was described as *'an informal and spontaneous gathering to consider the advisability of establishing a club to promote an interest in aquatic sport'.* Having agreed that the time was now ripe for the birth of such a club, a Provisional Sub-Committee was formed to draft rules, enrol members and obtain the necessary information in order to steer a course towards the eventual formation of a properly constituted club.

The twelve disciples of sailing present at this inaugural meeting of the steering group were: R J MacKintosh, R Maclean, Ian A Forsyth, Alex Macandie, Alex Urquhart, W J Cran, John Currie, W Davidson, Captain J McGregor, John Ross, D J Donald and John Robertson. Enlisting the support of a number of prominent figures among the landed gentry and the town and county councils, Invergordon Boating Club was formally constituted on 22nd July 1901 at a public meeting held in the Science and Art Rooms used by Invergordon Academy in what was then the Town Hall, the premises now occupied by the town library. The first office bearers were: President, Captain MacLeod of Cadboll; Vice-Presidents, Mr Urquhart of Delny, Mr Dyson Perrins of Ardross Castle (and of Lea and Perrins Worcester Sauce), Major MacKenzie of Dalmore, of the whisky distilling dynasty and Provost MacKenzie of Invergordon; Secretary was Mr Ian A Forsyth, Balintraid and Treasurer, Mr J Robertson, Bank Agent.

Ian A. Forsyth, Balintraid.
First Secretary of the Invergordon Boating Club, 1901-1907.

The committee enthusiastically made preparations for the first regatta which was to be held on 16 August, linking the event to the Annual Bazaar which was held to raise funds for the Nursing Service.

Reflecting the nature of much of the boating activity of the period and exercising the club's intention to encourage all forms of water sport, rowing as well as sailing races were organised. Mrs MacLeod of Cadboll, the President's wife, was invited to present the prizes and immediately responded by offering to present a trophy for open competition in sailing; the first winner was Mr Mackintosh of Thornbush, Inverness. The Class A prize of £1 10/- (£1.50 in present day currency) went to Mr John Ross of Invergordon and the cup presented by the Invergordon Town Council for rowing in four-oared boats was won by William Munro's pilot boat manned by A MacLean, W Bremner, D MacLeod and John Duff. A cash prize for two-oared boats was won by Murdo Gallie's boat manned by A MacLean and W Bremner. The event was a modest success with good weather and a considerable crowd assembling to watch the races but inexperience led to delays in starting races, this causing some dissatisfaction among spectators. The organisers clearly had lessons to learn in providing spectator appeal but subsequent events showed that these lessons were not ignored.

Encouraged by their success, plans were made for even more colourful events and in the years leading up to the First World War the Invergordon Boating Club Regatta was to become a major event in the summer social calendar.

As the Cromarty Firth was already being used regularly as an anchorage for the ships of the Royal Navy, it made sense to capitalise on this by holding the regatta when ships were in port. In 1902, the proposed date for the event was altered to coincide with a visit from the fishery protection cruiser, *HMS Jackal,* whose commanding officer, Captain Sharp, agreed to moor his ship 400 yards off the harbour. A line from the ship's bridge to a blue ensign flying on the west corner of the jetty served as the starting line, the firing of a gun signalling the start of the races. *Jackal's* boats were allowed to compete for the cash prizes in the rowing races, adding further interest to the competitions.

This arrangement appeared to be more successful. As *HMS Jackal* was not available in 1903, the beautiful steam yacht *Aphrodite* took on the role of starter. Owned by Colonel O. H. Payne, who had leased the shootings on Novar Estate, this elegant American-built ship lay at anchor in the firth for the duration of his stay. For his kindness Col Payne was subsequently invited to become a vice-president of the club.

This was the start of the Edwardian age, a time of considerable entrepreneurship and the ostentatious display of wealth, privilege and philanthropy and the committee showed commendable enterprise in eliciting the support of wealthy visitors and prominent local figures in providing services on the day of the regatta and the donation of trophies for competition.

In 1904 the three-masted schooner *Sunbeam,* in which Lord Brassey had travelled world-wide, arrived at Invergordon. Provost MacDonald and Mr J Robertson, the club treasurer, met with Lord Brassey on his yacht, resulting in his lordship expressing the desire to donate a silver trophy for competition.

Mr H W Ross, the Mayor of Salisbury, Rhodesia, and a native of Invergordon also presented a trophy, the Rhodesia Challenge Cup, for competition by boats belonging to owners within the Cromarty Firth. Both these trophies were won for the first time by Captain W MacKenzie of Dalmore. Captain Edwards of the yacht *Falcon* had come round from Inverness and offered his services for starting the races in the manner of previous years.

In 1905, invitations to become patrons of the club were accepted by Lord Brassey, the Countess of Moray, Mr S Munro of Teaninich, Major Stirling, Captain Featherstonhaugh and Andrew Carnegie, the Scot who had made an enormous fortune in the US steel industry and who now owned Skibo Castle on the shores of the Dornoch Firth. Elegant affluence was again in evidence with the presence once more of Col Payne's yacht *Aphrodite* and the Duke of Sutherland's steam yacht *Catania;* the honour of starting the races was granted to *Aphrodite* and Mrs Perrins of Ardross Castle agreed to present the prizes. Dressed with bunting, the ships presented a colourful spectacle for sightseers, their crews taking part in rowing races

Aphrodite.
Owned by Col Oliver H Payne of 5th Avenue, New York. Built in 1898 and sold to Greek owners in 1928.

Sunbeam.
A magnificent steam yacht built in 1874. Owned by Lord Brassey who became renowned for his famous circumnavigation of the World in 1876-77. Later presented by Lord Brassey to the Nautical College at Pangbourne in 1919.
Note: The funnel is stowed on the deck whilst under sail.

Interior Cabin onboard Sunbeam.
Extract from the Minute of August 16 1904. *"The Treasurer intimated that to date the club's funds amounted to £20:0:2: also that he and Provost Macdonald had called on Lord Brassey on board the 'Sunbeam' and that His Lordship had offered a silver cup to the club for competition."*

Falcon.
Capt. Edwards.

Catania.
Owned by Cromartie, 4th Duke of Sutherland. A beautiful Schooner built in 1895.

and other fun events which had been introduced to entertain spectators. These included racing in boats using shovels as oars, climbing the greasy pole which proved a great favourite with spectators and attracted a large number of competitors, tug-of-war in boats and swimming races.

Inspired by the growing success of the regatta, the committee boldly planned an even more spectacular event spanning two days for 1906.

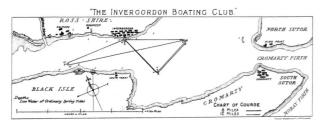

Chart of Course 1906.
Chart of the Race Course taken from the Boating Club 'Rules and Sailing Regulations Book' 1906.
Minute 16 October 1905: "It was referred to the committee to meet and draft new Rules and Regulations embracing the YRA Rules and get estimates for same."

Their efforts had not gone un-noticed; Mr Littlejohn of Invercharron, impressed with the club's encouragement of a healthy interest in a range of watersports, offered to present an impressive and valuable trophy for life-saving to be designated the Littlejohn of Invercharron Challenge Cup. It was accompanied by a deed of gift placing it in the trust of the Town Council, a visionary measure as, with changing circumstances, it is now competed for in the swimming pool at Invergordon Leisure Centre. Miss Ross of Invergordon, in memory of her late father Mr R S Ross who had been Town Clerk since 1878, presented the club with his yacht *Dolphin*. More trophies for the club's competitions were offered by the Duke of Sutherland, Mr G H Bankes of Balconie, Mr Walter Philip, the lessee of Invergordon Castle and the Dowager Countess of Moray who occupied Tarbet House at the time.

The real bonus, however, was the arrival in the firth of the ships of the Channel Fleet accompanied by a destroyer flotilla. Vice-Admiral Curzon-Howe offered the use of the forebridge of his flagship, the battleship *HMS Caesar*, for starting and provided hospitality to what the press described as *'a large and fashionable gathering of ladies and gentlemen from most of the leading county families and others*

HMS Caesar.
Motto: Veni Vidi Vici - I came, I saw, I conquered. Battleship of 14,900 tons built at Portsmouth, launched
in 1896. Sold for breaking up in Germany - 1921.

presently in the district' who had the privilege of viewing events from the deck of the flagship while being entertained by the ship's officers. The admiral also made another ship available to the general public as a viewing platform and the scene was set for the most spectacular regatta yet. The harbour, the large steam yachts and the ships of the fleet, all gaily decorated with flags, presented a magnificent spectacle and the sight of many small boats plying between the ships and the shore ensured there was plenty to excite the interest of the 2000 spectators who gathered for the event. The railway company had laid on special excursion trains and 700 passengers arrived on the steamship *James Crombie* from Lossiemouth. The first day dawned bright with a brisk breeze promising good conditions for sailing. Competition in the rowing races was keenly contested with entries from several boats from the ships of the fleet and the yacht *Aphrodite* whose crew excelled and won most of the rowing prizes.

The events included a comic element, not always intentional; in the competition for the Littlejohn of Invercharron Cup which stipulated that competitors had to be normally clothed and swim 75 yards to rescue another man in the water, Invergordon man Mr D Ross's interpretation was rather more literal than that of the other competitors. He wore heavy trousers and boots while the others were attired in light trousers and canvas shoes. A strong and confident swimmer, he was quite undettered by his handicap and finished only three or four yards behind the winner, drummer Fraser of the Seaforth Highlanders from Fort George. Steward Garnet Edwards of *HMS Caesar* demonstrated remarkable versatility by winning the 150 yards swimming race and then demonstrated matching proficiency by swimming vertically through almost frictionless grease to win the Greasy Pole competition. Conditions on the second day of the regatta were fine and sunny but an unfortunate lack of wind caused racing to be suspended. In spite of this setback there was no doubt that the event had been a considerable success and a major spectacle had been staged exciting yet more interest in the club.

Mr Wylie Hill of Lemlair presented another cup for plain-keeled open boats in August 1907 and gifted his boat *La Perita* to the club the following year.

Recognising the development of the internal combustion engine for small boats and in keeping with the club's aim of promoting all forms of water sport, motor boat races were introduced in 1909, Sir Kenneth Matheson of Lochalsh presenting a cup for this new competition. A series of fortnightly races for the Lady Moray Cup was inaugurated in 1911. In 1912 the two day format for the regatta was abandoned in favour of a one day event once more.

Chauvinism, which in these times was still politically respectable, was in a healthy state in Invergordon Boating Club. The club's rules allowed ladies to become members on payment of the membership fee but they were not allowed to vote. This was entirely consistent with the culture of the period; it was to be 1918 before women at least 30 years old gained the right to vote in parliamentary or local council elections and not until 1928 did women have the same voting rights as men.

In the summer of 1914, while the political storm in Europe raged over the assassination of Archduke Ferdinand of Austria in Sarajevo, the committee decided on 12 August as the date for the regatta.

On 3 August Britain declared war on Germany. The club's activities were suspended indefinitely.

Elf
Designed by Major W F Mackenzie of Dalmore on the shores of the Cromarty Firth on his return from the Boer War - c. 1902.

17

Chapter Three

The Inter-War Years 1925-1933

The club was resuscitated at a meeting chaired by Provost Ross of Invergordon Town Council on 3 September 1925 in the Town Hall. Major MacKenzie of Dalmore was elected President; Ian Forsyth of Balintraid, Vice-President and William George, the Town Clerk, Secretary. Following the pattern of previous years an impressive list of prominent names were included as Honorary Vice-Presidents and Patrons and a regatta, in the multi-activity format which had proved successful in the pre-war years, was planned for 14 August 1926. Their enthusiasm was rewarded by a successful and well-organised event. The press described the weather as delightful and the demonstrations of water polo and life-saving in the harbour by members of Inverness Amateur Swimming Club added interest for the large crowd of spectators who lined both piers. Among the prizewinning boats were *Elf* and *Petunia,* which had clearly suffered no ill effects from the long absence of competitive sailing in the intervening years, these vessels having been frequent winners in the earlier years of the club's existence.

Encouraged by the resurgence of interest, the committee met on the night of the regatta and immediately agreed to plan the next regatta for 1927. The railway company was approached to offer cheap day excursions from as far away as Keith and Helmsdale and a naval diving team from *HMS Moorfowl* was invited to provide a demonstration of underwater diving.

Invergordon Boating Club 14th August 1926.

Baillie J.E. McDONALD EARL OF CRAVEN Wm. GEORGE
Ex PROVOST JOHN MCDONALD ROBERT MUNRO Maj A.W. BROOK

Described as one of the most successful regattas ever, on a day of glorious sunshine with a light cooling breeze, the spectators were well entertained, not least by one of the fun events, a mock barber shop staged on a raft in the middle of the harbour. Here *'shampooing, shaving, shingling, bingling and Eton Crops'* were inflicted on volunteers whose reward for subjecting themselves to the burlesque treatment was to be ceremoniously tipped into the chill waters of the harbour. All races were keenly contested but the handicapping system caused some perplexity for spectators; in the motor boat race, in which nine boats took part over a keenly watched eight mile course, the boat which crossed the line last was declared the winner on handicap, prompting the Ross-shire Journal to ask that handicaps be made known to the public in order to further their understanding of events. On this occasion, the Lord Brassey Trophy for open sailing left the firth for the first time bound for Findhorn on board Mr Chisholm's yacht, *Humbug*. Once again there was no doubt that a hard working committee had staged yet another major visitor attraction and such was the euphoria after the event

that the Ross-shire Journal proclaimed: *'The Invergordon Regatta has come to stay.'*

The omens certainly looked promising with an estimated crowd of over 5000 turning up at the harbour again in 1928. The steamship *Ailsa* which had brought passengers from Nairn and Cromarty, offered cheap excursions throughout a day of brilliant sunshine with a light breeze. The Cromarty Lifeboat crew gave a demonstration of lifesaving; Mr and Mrs Allan from Aberdeen gave a demonstration of swimming and diving; a team of highland dancers performed on a raft in the middle of the harbour and the pipe bands of Invergordon and Inverness LMS Boy Scouts played stirring music throughout the day. The enlarged programme of races for sailing, rowing, motor boats, the swimming races, lifesaving competition, demonstrations and fun events certainly justified the Ross-shire Journal's headline *'Magnificent Spectacle at Harbour'*.

No mention of any weekly club races appears in the club records of this period until 1930; yet such races would appear to have been taking place as it is recorded that a cup was to be purchased for the

S.S. Ailsa.

The Royal Mail Steamship *Ailsa* was part of the romantic scene of the Cromarty Firth in the 1920s and 1930s. John Watson was Captain of the *'Ailsa'* and for many years he was also Coxswain of the Cromarty Lifeboat.

Photo: Eric Malcolm - Cromarty 1933 - 1936.

Cromarty Lifeboats.
RNLB *'Lilla Marass Douglas and Will'*
1955 - 1968.
(Left)

RNLB *'James Macfee'*
1928 - 1955.
(Right)

Photo: Clem Watson RNLI (Rtd)

weekly sailing competitions starting in June of that year and that these would be changed from Saturdays to Wednesdays.

There can be no doubt that club members took advantage of the firth to hone their skills and tune their boats for the kind of performance that wins trophies at regattas, but whatever organised or informal sailing was taking place, the focus of the club's efforts remained the grand public spectacle of the regatta which always attracted large numbers of spectators and enhanced the lives of the men of the Royal Navy whose crews participated keenly when their ships were in port.

The arrival of the fleet was of enormous social and economic importance with up to 20000 men having to be fed and entertained. Fun fairs and street stalls, coconut shies and sideshows were set up on shore as complementary attractions to the regatta; the Black Isle ferries, railway company and pleasure steamers all capitalised on the attractions of the day providing cruises around the ships of the fleet. Dances and sporting events were staged to provide recreation; in the evenings thirsty ratings filled the local public houses while the officers enjoyed the hospitality offered at many country house parties. Local farmers and shops prospered, supplying vegetables, meat and clothing and, of course, when the sailors were in port there were also a number of enterprising ladies ready to profit from the occasion. Such was the demand that the local talent had to be complemented by reinforcements from as far away as London, an annual migration towards Invergordon which prompted one local observer to remark, 'They'll be here, even on crutches'. These were colourful days indeed.

On 8 May 1931, Mr William Martineau of Kincraig House, one of the club's patrons, was invited to become the club's first Commodore. In response to this honour, he offered to present a cup for the senior race for class A boats together with a Commodore's Flag which the winner would have the privilege of flying for a year. Presented at the 1931 regatta, it was won for the first time by Major Mackenzie of Dalmore in *Mascot*. After a dull morning the sun shone throughout the afternoon and a fine day's sport was enjoyed. A star guest was Piper Laidlaw VC of the 7th King's Own Scottish Borderers; the award of the Victoria Cross for his courage at the Battle of Loos in 1915 had earned him the status of a national hero. The sight and sound of his kilted figure parading openly along the parapet of the trenches, playing his pipes while under constant enemy fire, inspired his comrades into attack on the enemy lines and, in spite of being cut down and wounded by gun fire, he continued to play on until the position was secured. Now, his playing inspired the dancers on the raft in the harbour and he also accompanied the Boy Scouts Pipe Band. *'Year by year the Invergordon Regatta is becoming more popular',* trumpeted the Ross-shire Journal, proclaiming the 1931 regatta as the *'Best on Record'.*

The regatta may have been completed in an afternoon of beautiful sunshine but a chill breeze was blowing in the corridors of power; Mr J E MacDonald had resigned as President, Mr William George OBE, the Town Clerk, who as secretary of the club had put in an enormous amount of work behind the scenes in organising these events for the past five years, had also resigned earlier in the year due to pressure of public duties. Mr George was presented with a clock in recognition of his stalwart

service to the club and Mr F MacKay of the Commercial Bank took over as Secretary. Coincidentally, the appointment of an assistant secretary is perhaps indicative of the workload involved.

A study of the secretary's correspondence at this time reveals much about the labour involved in setting up such a big event; dealing with people from outside the club as well as coordinating the efforts of the host of helpers required from within, organising transport, policing, advertising and, in particular, the difficulties experienced in cajoling entries for events in advance of the day demonstrated that his task was not without its frustrations. In letters written to Inverness and Nairn swimming clubs soliciting swimming entries to swell the numbers and to Findhorn Yacht Club to encourage more entries for sailing races, a sense of despair is evident. *'I admit being a bit disheartened at not only the number of entries, but at the habit they have of not entering till the day of the sports, leaving me in doubt as to whether or not there will be any sports at all.'*

However, Mr MacKay's efforts paid off and the

scene was set for another glorious day's competition in 1932, advertising *'thirteen magnificent silver cups for races, the Littlejohn of Invercharron Life-Saving Cup with accompanying gold, silver and bronze medals, exhibitions of waterpolo, graceful diving and swimming by ladies and gentlemen and comic stunts'.* Cromarty Lifeboat was again in attendance. Captain Albert Watson of the ss *Ailsa* again brought spectators from Nairn and Cromarty and ran afternoon trips for sightseers; trains, buses and the ferry boats from the Black Isle brought more. Sailors from *HMS Moorfowl* staged slap-stick comic events entitled 'The Arrest of Ghandi', 'The Battle of the Millers and Sweeps' and 'Dr Sawbones' as well as an exhibition of deep sea diving. Three yachts made the trip over from Findhorn and did not go home empty-handed, Lord Brassey's Cup taking another trip east at the end of the day. All the races were keenly contested with a large number of entrants and it all took place once again in the perfect weather which now seemed an ever-present feature of the Invergordon Regatta.

But however successful it appeared on the day, the machinery required to stage such a show was grinding uncomfortably towards a crisis. The telephone was not yet a common instrument of communication, so much time was spent writing letters and waiting for responses, these often requiring further follow-up letters. While many people responded well by giving willing support on the day, there was a marked reluctance to become involved in the detailed planning which was fundamental to the success of such a large event and in April 1933 Mr MacKay announced that he could not continue as secretary.

On 9 May it was recorded that three un-named gentlemen were approached to take over as secretary but none was willing to undertake the duties. A further effort was made to recruit a secretary with the added inducement of an honorarium but this too failed to produce a positive response and, as no member was willing to accept this essential office, it was decided to cancel the proposed regatta for 1933. A sub-committee was appointed to try to engage a secretary for the following year but met with no success. Mr MacKay's final duty was to collect all trophies belonging to the club and to lodge them in the bank for safe keeping.

The regatta, though it had become such a popular and colourful event, was certainly not here to stay; at least not in the style established in these early years of the club's existence. While sailors undoubtedly would have continued to sail on the firth in the years leading up to the Second World War, there is no evidence of any club activity or organised competition in that period.

During the war the firth saw less of a naval presence than previously. The Cromarty Firth was within range of enemy bombers and the success of the Japanese attack on Pearl Harbour exposed the vulnerability of shipping to torpedo attacks by bombers. However, its sheltered stretch of water made it an ideal base for the flying boats of the RAF based at Alness and the flat land on its shores provided for war-time airfields at Evanton, Fearn and Tain.

In the post war years, the RAF presence which continued at Alness until the early 1980s and at the base at Kinloss would provide fresh competition for the club. The naval presence declined after the war; although ships did still visit, it was never on quite the same scale as before.

Chapter Four

The Postwar Years 1948-1965

The next recorded meeting in the club's minute book is dated 9 February 1948 when the club was reformed at a meeting in the Council Chambers. Hugh Ross was elected President and F Carter, Secretary, with 25 members being enrolled.

On its second re-birth the club adopted an approach consistent with the change in culture and lifestyle which followed the Second World War; gone were the days of seeking the patronage of the wealthy and attempting to provide a big show for spectators. Any attempt to resuscitate the regatta in its previous form would almost certainly have been doomed to failure; society had changed and was finding more sophisticated ways of entertaining itself.

This was a period of expansion in water sports. Many young men were introduced to the sport through national service; the Army, Navy and RAF all had their own sailing clubs which, in peacetime, provided opportunities for teamwork, adventure and challenge for active young men and women. Yacht builders still provided elegant cruisers and racers built in wood for those who could afford them, but new production techniques and materials being developed would mean that the DIY sailing dinghy would soon have its day, making sailing accessible to a much wider section of the population. Motor power had superseded oars as a practical means of propelling small boats for commercial or pleasurable activity and rowing was a dying art; the days of the rowing races were numbered.

The club now focussed primarily on racing under sail and at its first meeting took steps to identify and procure boats and dinghies which were believed to be available. Colonel Ian Anderson offered the club the use of his boat *Priscilla* for the season; Mr Watson of Clyde Street agreed to provide instruction on boat handling to club members and contact was made with the Findhorn and Beauly yacht clubs seeking their cooperation during this first season. A regatta was arranged in August 1948, a much more modest affair than those of the past, with a programme of sailing races for three classes. The Class A boats, over 20 feet overall, included two old club stalwarts which had been sailing now for almost half a century; *Elf,* owned by Mr Hugh Ross, Lochslin, and *Petunia,* now owned by Col Ross of Cromarty. Major HAC MacKenzie in *Mascot* was the only other competitor in this class. Only two boats were entered in Class B, 17 to 20 feet overall; *Shamwari* of Beauly and *Wandering Boy* from Findhorn. Class C races for boats under 17 feet was another two-horse race involving Mr Ian Moodie's *Kathleen* and *Mr Pooh,* a small RNSA clinker-built dinghy owned by the King's Harbourmaster, Commander Westmacott. Unspectacular compared with past regattas, it was nevertheless the start of a period characterised by an adventurous, enthusiastic involvement in yacht racing with some cruising as well. The focus had shifted from putting on a show to having fun messing about in boats.

The weather appears to have changed too. The glorious days with gentle breezes which had characterised the regattas in the twenties and thirties had given way to strong winds and blustery conditions, providing thrills and spills aplenty. In 1949 one of the boats sailed by the Moodie Brothers from Evanton broke her tiller and capsized;

the lads were rescued by the ferryboat which towed their boat ashore where it was bailed out and sailed again. *Petunia,* perhaps showing her age at last, also broke her rudder and was forced to withdraw. In spite of the conditions a motor boat race and a rowing race were also held.

The Cromarty Regatta had better fortune however and Invergordon boats performed well there with *Elf, Petunia* and *Mr Pooh* all collecting silverware. Press reports now included results of the weekly series of races, demonstrative of an enthusiastic and active membership. There was no lack of excitement either at the regatta in July 1950; on a blustery day with a strong south easterly wind which provided challenging conditions, two capsizes and two dis-mastings were reported. Rescue cover was provided by RAF Kinloss with converted airborne lifeboats and a heartening entry of 20 yachts was reported. A special race was arranged for the RAF's converted airborne lifeboats whose crews demonstrated exceptional skill in boat handling. These lifeboats were slung underneath search and rescue aircraft for dropping to survivors of planes which had ditched in the sea. A further

*Invergordon boats on the start line
at Cromarty Regatta in 1965.*

John Forsyth's converted RAF Airborne Lifeboat.

regatta was held a month later. This time the weather was much kinder, being described as ideal for racing and the event attracted what was reported as a good crowd of spectators.

1951 was a year of change. The club changed its title to Invergordon Sailing Club but there is no evidence that any account was taken of the implications of this, a matter which was to raise its head a decade later regarding the ownership of the club trophies which had been presented to Invergordon Boating Club.

Undeterred by such matters, the members were having fun, their growing enthusiasm being reflected in the arrival of several new boats on the scene. Hugh Ross moved up from his faithful and successful *Elf* to a larger boat, *Ulva*. Press reports indicate that he sailed the boat up from Rothesay with Richard Brooke of Cromarty Mains as crew, having competed and won prizes at regattas in the Clyde and Forth. Major HAC Mackenzie acquired *White Heather* from Findhorn; Ian Ross, *Red Wing;* Ian Moodie, *Why Not;* and Major Forsyth, *Adenach,* all for the 1951 season. Again the conditions on the day of the regatta proved testing with no shortage of thrills. *Elf* and *Petunia* both capsized, breaking rudders and withdrawing; rescues were effected by RAF speedboats and the Invergordon ferryboat skippered by Dougal Mackintosh, a club stalwart who had been a successful competitor in earlier years.

In this post-war era the female voice began to be heard in the affairs of the club. The fact that females could be capable of sailing boats as well as making tea and sandwiches was accorded some recognition in 1952. The AGM, with 25 un-named members present, agreed to a proposal, from whom it is not recorded, that a ladies race be held. Now whether or not the ladies were interested in participating in races on equal terms with the men remains uncertain but the minute of the meeting records: *'A Ladies Race was proposed on any day convenient to them.'* Chauvinism was still alive and well.

If a polite murmur of rebelliousness had been heard from the ladies of the club, a full testosterone-laden roar was heard from the men with regard to the problems experienced in obtaining land for dinghy stowage. On 2 July, with understandable anguish,

Fairwind.

Petunia   *White Heather*
Ariel   *Red Wing*

the secretary reported on his efforts to obtain permission to store dinghies on a few square yards of land to the east of the swimming pool which was demolished in the 1970s to make way for the new harbour ring road. The matter had been taken up with the Town Council, then referred to The Ministry of Town and Country Planning, passed on to The Minister of Crown Lands and finally to The Ministry of Transport. It is recorded that members *'expressed disgust at this absurd bureaucratic nonsense and, if no reply were obtained within a week, the club would go ahead, build the pen and await developments'.* Happily, on 9 August, the secretary was able to report that the Minister of Crown Lands had agreed to the building of a dinghy pen on the foreshore at a rent of £1 per year.

Cromarty Firth c1950s.
Naval Vessels : Pleasure Sailing : Commercial Shipping.

Flying Boats
beyond the pool.

By Invergordon
Swimming Pool

Yet another new vessel, the six metre dragon class sloop *Aerielle,* purchased by Richard Brooke of Cromarty was sailed up from Glasgow by himself, Hugh Ross and HAC MacKenzie and was one of 18 boats from Invergordon, Cromarty and Findhorn competing in the regatta, this time held in brilliant weather.

Good Friends.
At the Caledonian Canal on way home from the West.
Hugh Ross : Richard Brooke : HAC Mackenzie.

Mr Murchison's boat Rhona.

However, the mishaps which had dogged recent regattas continued; Ian Ross's boat *Red Wing* collided with Alness schoolmaster J Murchison's *Rhona* and *Rhona* broke her mast. *Mr Pooh*, skippered by Commander Westmacott, capsized and the Queen's Harbourmaster and his crew had to be rescued by the ferryboat which towed his boat ashore.

Invergordon yachts were now travelling further and achieving success in other events; *Ulva,* with Hugh Ross, Richard Brooke and Ian Moodie aboard, competed successfully in the Oban Regatta and Major HAC MacKenzie refused to let bad weather prevent him from taking part in the Findhorn Regatta. While other local boats were unable to make the crossing in difficult sea conditions, he hoisted his boat, *White Heather,* on to the back of a lorry and made the trip by road. His enthusiasm was rewarded; *White Heather* won her class race and returned triumphantly with a silver pennant.

An eventful season of turbulent weather continued with an all-comers yacht race held on 30 August when the ships of the Home Fleet were in port, with nine dinghies from the fleet taking part. And in yet another September race with several whalers from *HMS Widmouth Bay* joining the racing, strong squalls ripped the sails of several yachts and one boat was driven ashore.

Misfortune struck again in the last race of the 1954 season when Ian Ross's yacht, *Red Wing* ran aground on a sandbank on the Black Isle side of the firth. *Ulva* went to the rescue and Hugh Ross and his crew anchored near the stricken vessel and sent a dinghy alongside with a rope. Both yachts then hoisted sails and *Ulva* towed *Red Wing* clear of the sandbank in a fine feat of seamanship. In 1955 the intrepid Hugh Ross set off in *Ulva* to compete again in the Oban Regatta. Undeterred by draught restrictions imposed in the Caledonian Canal at the time, Hugh took the long and perilous route round the North of Scotland through the turbulent tide races of the Pentland Firth and round Cape Wrath in what may have been the first time a club boat took this route - a route still navigated, understandably, by only a relatively small number of club skippers.

After such a lively and adventurous rebirth, the club appeared to slip into decline in the late fifties and

Prize Winners in the 1950s.
Hugh Ross : Brian Peck? : Unknown : Ian Legge
Unknown : Jay : Richard Brooke : Ken MacPherson

Young lads from Invergordon encouraged to take up sailing in their early years.
Hamish (Skipper) Ross : Dennis Mellon : Gordon Legge

early sixties. It had been running fairly informally for some years; Ron Stewart remembers that in the late fifties the regatta was organised by a few club members meeting at the pier on the morning just prior to the event, a far cry from the burdening administration of the late twenties period. Club records at this time are scant. The only entries in the minute book since 1952 were brief minutes of the Annual General Meetings until 1958; the next entry is in 1963 when, with 19 people present, many of them non-members, it was hoped that this would '*indicate a resurgence of interest and that they would apply to join the club'*. However, there is no record of any other activity in the minute book until 1965 when 8 members met in the House of Rosskeen to discuss a proposal of a merger with Invergordon Aquatic Club.

Chapter Five

The New Age 1966-1981

In the 1950s the boat owners of the Sailing Club had been mainly landowning farmers and self employed businessmen; crews were recruited from among those with an interest in sailing but who could not afford a boat. However, after the economic austerity in the immediate post-war years, the country experienced a period of significant social and economic change during the fifties. Wages were improving, car and home ownership were expanding rapidly and more leisure time was available to more people; this was the age that coined the phrase by Prime Minister Harold MacMillan, *'You've never had it so good'*. And a series of events of considerable historical, industrial and scientific importance extending over a long period of time were now bringing the cost of boat ownership and maintenance within the reach of a much wider section of the population.

It all started with the French Revolution in 1789. Just before the storming of the Bastille, Pierre DuPont, a publisher and writer, had allegedly shown a distinct lack of foresight in declaring his support for the doomed monarchy and had to flee to America. His family proved more visionary and in 1802 started trading in gunpowder; with the colonisation of the American West getting underway this proved to be a shrewd move. The DuPont business quickly became one of the leading industrial dynasties of the age and has been in continuous production ever since. Expanding into textile production, DuPont recognised the threat posed by the British firm of Courtaulds who began manufacturing stockings made of Rayon, an artificial silk, in 1885. These, however, were baggy and uncomfortable to wear but the search for a man-made fibre was on and DuPont invested heavily in fundamental scientific research. Meanwhile mineral oil, which had first been drilled in earnest in Pennsylvania in 1859, was to become probably the most important raw material of the 20th century, influencing political and social developments, as scientists discovered a multitude of petroleum derivatives. DuPont's investment paid off handsomely. Neoprene, synthetic rubber, was produced in 1933 and one of the scientists funded by DuPont synthesised from the raw materials petroleum, natural gas, water and air, a new material which was to change the world. A new word was born, Nylon, which was launched commercially in 1938. Polyester followed in 1941. By the 1960s derivatives of these products had proliferated. Nylon, terylene, polyesters, PVC, polypropylene, polyethylene, velcro, GRP, all became integrated into nautical language; materials which are now found in the hulls, decks, rigging and fittings of modern boats and in the gear worn by sailors. Strong, durable, lightweight, resistant to rot and relatively inexpensive, these innovations brought about a revolution in boat building, a reduction in maintenance costs and an explosion of activity in sailing, motor boating, diving, waterskiing and the birth of sailboarding.

And so the Invergordon Aquatic Club was born. It had been established in 1963 with Bill Smith, Principal Teacher of Technical Subjects at Invergordon Academy, as Commodore and its constitution was closely aligned with the original constitution of Invergordon Boating Club, stating that the club's object was *'to promote, encourage and facilitate aquatic sports'*. The original Boating Club constitution had as the object of the club, the encouragement of boat sailing and rowing, to which was added swimming after the presentation of the Littlejohn of Invercharron Lifesaving Trophy in 1904. Drawing its membership from a wider spectrum than the Sailing Club, the Aquatic Club members were dinghy sailors, speed boat owners and a few waterskiers.

Although the Aquatic Club had some trophies of its own, it is reported by one of the founding members that this club tried to obtain the trophies which had previously been in the possession of the Invergordon Boating Club, now Invergordon Sailing Club, and which, due to the lack of activity had been lodged in the bank. This request had, however, been denied by the bank as the trophies had originally been awarded to Invergordon Boating Club and could therefore only be released to a club constituted under that name. The Aquatic Club proposed a merger of the two clubs. At a Sailing Club committee meeting held in Rosskeen House in April 1965, with only four members present, a merger was agreed subject to certain conditions, one of which was that the joint club title be Invergordon Sailing Club. This proposal was, however, untenable. The reversion to the original title was essential, together with the documentary evidence of a new constitution, in order to obtain release of the trophies from the vaults of the bank. A deputation consisting of Hugh Ross, Major HAC MacKenzie and Cdr Elwin from the Sailing Club met with representatives of the Aquatic Club to discuss their proposals for merging the two clubs and the first general meeting of the re-formed Invergordon Boating Club was held on 17 May 1965.

Commander Elwin, the Queen's Harbourmaster, was elected Commodore; John Burgess, Vice Commodore; Bill Smith, Rear Commodore; M MacLennan, Secretary and Miss S McIntosh, Treasurer, became the club's first female office-bearer. A new constitution was drawn up and the trophies put in trust. A Sailing Committee consisting of D Mackintosh, E Howell and M MacLennan was elected and the RYA was informed of the amalgamation of the two clubs.

This was the age of the sailing dinghy with the ubiquitous GP 14 and Mirror dinghies battling for supremacy, boats which good design, modern materials and construction techniques had brought within affordable range of most enthusiasts. Within a couple of years races were being run on Wednesdays, Saturdays and Sundays, with occasional motor boat races, as well as the annual regatta. Membership was growing and, with a vision of their own clubhouse and dinghy park in mind, members engaged in a range of fund-raising schemes. By 1968 negotiations were in hand to acquire the title to land at Shore Road at the head of the old ferry slip for a clubhouse and dinghy pen.

But on the political and industrial stage the curtain had already been raised on a series of dramas which would have a profound effect on the club and bring about the most dynamic period of change in its history.

In October 1967 at the Labour Party Conference, Prime Minister Harold Wilson announced plans for two new aluminium smelters, one of which would shortly be built at Invergordon. A massive programme of construction began, creating not only the smelter but also hundreds of new houses to accommodate the influx of new families it brought to the area. This growth in population meant potential recruits; incoming workers, young people, teachers, doctors and others involved in the infrastructure supporting the industrial development. New members arrived, some with considerable experience of sailing, who were to play an important role in helping the club establish itself as a force for the remainder of the century.

Even more significant was the effect of the discovery of oil in the North Sea. In 1972, work started on the construction of the fabrication yard for oil production platforms at Nigg Bay which would employ around 6000 workers at its peak. Shortly afterwards, a pipe coating plant was developed at Saltburn. By this time, oil-rig supply vessels were using the harbour at Invergordon regularly and the potential of the Cromarty Firth with its deep sheltered water as a major centre for supply, repair and maintenance of exploration rigs was recognised. Major development of the harbour was inevitable and the Cromarty Firth Port Authority was established in 1974 with far reaching implications for Invergordon Boating Club.

While all this was developing, club members had been busy acquiring the land for a club base and had started building their dinghy pen in 1969; gates were obtained from Invergordon Distillery and in 1972 a hut, surplus to requirements after the construction of the smelter, was acquired. However, by the time the club had occupied its new base it was already under threat by the proposed development of the harbour area as a supply base for the North Sea oil industry. The harbour required extension in order to meet the growing need for deep water berths, storage and servicing facilities for the oil industry, an extension which would consume the property the club had obtained. The club had scarcely moved in when it had to consider the prospect of moving out again; in the next few years officials would be required to devote considerable time and energy in a series of prolonged negotiations involving the Port Authority, Highland Regional Council, the Highlands and Islands Development Board, RYA, local councillor Mrs Isobel Rhind and Hamish Gray MP. Major issues of concern included not only the acquisition of a new site for a clubhouse, but also the enclosure and restrictions on use of the west harbour and the proposed Port Authority Bye Laws, particularly regarding recreational use of the firth by pleasure craft. The effort involved during this turbulent period is clearly demonstrated by the enormous volume of correspondence, discussions and consultations noted in the club's records.

A huge debt is owed to those officials of the club whose indefatigable efforts over many years, in often troubled negotiations, secured the future of the club and access to the firth for recreation, acquired funding, prepared designs and saw through to completion the erection of the clubhouse it now occupies at Rosskeen. In this regard special recognition must be given to the efforts of the club commodores of the period, Donald Stevenson, Duncan Murray, and Douglas Young, the latter two also serving as secretary at various times and Isobel Bruce who served as treasurer for many years. Their monument exists in the clubhouse built by Alness Construction, whose tender of £22,453.37 was accepted in 1979 to a design by local architects, Thoms-Wilkie Partnership.

The club moved into its new premises on 2 May 1981. The clubhouse was formally opened by former Commodore Ian Ross who had been made an honorary member of the club in 1980 in recognition of his many years of service and, in recognition of their services to the building of the clubhouse, Donald Stevenson and Andy Thoms were made honorary members at the AGM in 1982.

Despite the difficulties experienced during this period the club continued to extend its activities. The boom in the production of GRP yachts brought larger boats within the reach of more people and, reflecting the growing number of cruising yachts in the area, the Moray Firth Cruiser Race between Findhorn and Cromarty was born in 1973 and has since become one of the leading events in the North of Scotland racing calendar.

Recognising the risks associated with the increase in shipping and boating activity in the inner Moray Firth area, the RNLI proposed setting up a new lifeboat station at Invergordon in October 1973 at a meeting in the Council Chambers. A significant number of club members volunteered as crew members for the lifeboat which has been well

Annual Prizegiving c 1975.
Bob Nicholson   Mardie Murray   Duncan Murray
Donald Stevenson   Bill Lynas   John Clark   David Bruce

Social Function.
In the 1970s members and friends travelled by boat to the
Annual Prizegiving and Dance at the Royal Hotel, Cromarty.

served by members of the club since the station was first commissioned. David Lipp retired as cox in 1999 after 25 years service, 18 of these as coxswain; Sandy Mackenzie served as 2nd Coxswain for many years and many others served and still serve the RNLI. This close association led to joint activities at Open Days and the institution of races for the RNLI pennant with the proceeds raised going to the lifeboat funds.

The club's state of health may be judged by the membership figures which in 1974 stood at 52 members of which 12 were junior members, an encouraging trend for the future, and a total of 378 boats started in 16 series of races on Wednesdays, Saturdays and Sundays during the season. With the opening of the Cromarty Firth Bridge in 1979 and the Kessock Bridge in 1982 club membership now became accessible to people from a wider catchment area, rising to 80 in 1980, by which time the ownership of boats was now balanced more or less equally between dinghies and cruisers.

Club location at ferry slip by the Harbour.

Invergordon Lifeboat.
Past and present members of Invergordon Boating Club.
Iain Armstrong, Andrew Murray & Danny Coutts.
Photo: Ross-shire Journal

Donald Stevenson. Commodore 1978 - 1980.
Guided the Club over the construction of the new Clubhouse
and awarded honorary membership in light of his generosity.

Chapter Six

Coming of Age 1982-2001

This was the era of the oil rig. With the expansion of the harbour area and the subsequent construction of the Queen's Dock, the Cromarty Firth was ready to become a major centre for the inspection, maintenance and repair of drilling rigs; depending on the fluctuations in drilling activity up to 17 rigs could be seen moored in the firth. This had implications, not only for safety, but also for the courses the club could set for racing and the early eighties were dominated by the continuing negotiations with the Port Authority on the Port Authority Bye Laws. It was incumbent on the club to ensure that its members behaved responsibly and, with new and sometimes inexperienced members, the next few years were characterised by an upsurge of training activity.

A winter programme of events was organised which included illustrated talks presented by the RYA and a lecture by transatlantic rower and Round The World Sailor and adventurer, John Ridgway MBE. Club members shared their experiences in the interest of advancing proficiency with slide shows of cruises in the Greek islands by Alastair Bulman and on the West of Scotland by Bill Robb. Keith Stanley, a yachtsman of considerable experience who had built the remarkably fast trimaran, *Boadicea,* provided offshore training on navigation, safety and the practical problems of cruising in all weather conditions. Patrick Moriarty gave a lecture on safety equipment and clothing and Tom Pollock, who was later to represent Scotland in the World Topper Championships in Norway, gave a helpful lecture on racing tactics. Duncan Murray delivered a course on the duties of Officers of the Day prior to the commencement of club racing and, on the water, Dennis Slattery provided dinghy training for junior members. A novel event introduced by Keith Stanley in the spring of 1983 was an overnight race in the Moray Firth ending with breakfast in the clubhouse at Invergordon; other moonlight races were held in subsequent years.

In 1984 the club had become a RYA Approved Training Centre; 20 students enrolled in evening classes for Yachtmaster, Day Skipper and Coastal

Sagacious.
Winner of the year 2000 Moray Firth Cruiser Race.
Skippered by Andrew Murray with crew members Terry MacLeod and Mark Robson.

The Moray Firth Cruiser Race.

Skipper qualifications in Alness Academy led by tutor Sandy MacKenzie, these classes becoming an established feature of the club's activity to the present day. In later years Sandy also provided training for the VHF Radio Certificate, Power Boat Handling and Rescue Boat Operation and in the late nineties Dr Jackson delivered training for First Aid qualifications.

In 1984, sailing sessions were provided by Ron Stewart and George Shields for 16 Ross-shire Girl Guides and Rangers; sessions were also organised for blind sailors and Milton Youth Club. The 1985 summer programme of training for dinghy sailors, led by Sandy MacKenzie, attracted 18 junior members and a number of adults. By this time a new class of sailor had evolved; the sailboarder. Sailboarders were accepted into membership of the club and two races were offered in the programme for the 1984 regatta. An Open Day was held in 1985 and attracted more new members in spite of an overloaded club rescue boat capsizing in blustery conditions, fortunately only a few yards from the slipway. That year the regatta attracted 18 sailboarders from as far afield as Burghead, Nairn

and Loch Ness thanks to the enthusiasm of Councillor Lou Wilkerson who had rallied support from this insurgent interest group. By the end of 1985 club membership had reached 91, 10 of these being sailboarders. In 1986 Invergordon Sea Cadets became a member organisation. The extent of these activities is indicative of the enthusiasm and support members were giving one another, surely a measure of a successful club and was reflected in the performances of club sailors in the race results of regattas in the North of Scotland and beyond.

The encouragement of junior members and the effectiveness of the club's training programme were evident in the results of the various regattas in which they competed. In the 1984 Highland Schools Regatta at Fortrose, Julie Mardon and Catriona Campbell won the Mirror Class races, Mark Robson and Colin Murray coming home overall winners in the Handicap Class. In the annual Nigg Cup race from Invergordon to Cromarty in 1985, Julie Mardon and Catriona Campbell won in splendid fashion, surging down the firth to Cromarty in their Mirror, the smallest boat in the fleet, with Terry Macleod and Colin Murray in a 420 taking second place and Mark Denny in a GP 14 third. Terry Macleod and Colin Murray also won the Oreco Sailing Scholarship at Findhorn and up at Scrabster Mark Robson won the slow handicap prize at the Pentland Firth Regatta. Colin Murray's early training was to stand him in good stead after joining the Royal Marines where he quickly established himself as the regiment's leading sailor. His older brother Andrew became the youngest ever winner of the Moray Firth Cruiser Race at the age of 19. Competing in a fleet of 30 yachts over a 40 mile course from Findhorn to Cromarty and skippering his father Duncan's boat, *Even Up,* his crew for the day were even younger; Mark Robson and Terry Macleod were both only 17 years old.

The senior members were doing not too badly either. After coming second in 1981 and third in 1982, Tom Pollock became the 1983 Scottish Champion in the Topper Class and represented his country in the World Championships held in Norway, the first Invergordon Boating Club member to gain international recognition. Keith

Stanley's three-hulled flyer *Boadicea* left the rest of the fleet behind in the darkness in an overnight race to the Beatrice Oil Field, arriving back at Findhorn in the morning to win the Findhorn Club's Varis Cup. The same boat in the Scottish Islands and Peaks Race logged the fastest time in the Arran to Largs section of the race. Several skippers including Donnie MacDonald, Andy Thoms, Duncan Murray, Martin Ryan, George Shields, George O'Hara, David Vass and Peter Cheyne frequently combined cruising with racing, bringing home silverware from regattas on the Clyde, Oban, Orkney and Shetland. *Sagacious,* skippered by Duncan Murray has gained a formidable reputation, winning 1st prize in the Fleetwood race at Lossiemouth in 1999 and has performed well in the McEwans Scottish Series at Tarbert Loch Fyne. In 1994 George O'Hara entered his boat *Coffee Cream* in the Mobile North Sea Race from Banff to Stavanger, performing well in very difficult sea conditions. Invergordon Boating Club skippers have had notable success in the Moray Firth Cruiser Race since its inception. Now a three class race, the list of Invergordon winners is impressive and probably unmatched by any other club with *Express, Quackers, Coffee Cream, Egret, Sagacious,* and *Fija* all winning class trophies in the past few years with *Sagacious* a three times winner in this period. In 1994, the first ten places in a fleet of twenty one Class A boats were taken by Invergordon boats with *Quackers* winning and in 1997 *Sagacious* romped home first with IBC fellow club skipper Martyn Ryan aboard *"Shamrock"* taking second place. In the 2000 race, the winners in all three classes were IBC boats with Duncan Murray's *Sagacious* taking the class A prize, Peter Cheyne's *Egret* was the class B winner and Lennie MacKay in *Fija* completed this notable hatrick by taking home the class C trophy. IBC has had a similar record in the North of Scotland 7 Series winning almost every year. This competition was renamed the Tomatin Series following a sponsorship deal with Tomatin Distillery in 1994. It is now sponsored by Caley Marina and is held at Lossiemouth over three consecutive days, offering a different variety of races.

Sponsorship of sporting events by business and industry was now commonplace. In the early years of the club's existence it had relied for support on the patronage of the wealthy classes. Philanthropy was now exercised in the form of support from the commercial sector. In the past 25 years of the club's existence it has received support in kind from companies such as Invergordon Distillery, Taylor Wrightson, Caley Marina and received an injection of cash for the upkeep of the rescue boat from The Beatrice Trust, set up by Britoil. In spite of the sometimes tense relationship with the Port Authority it has been supportive of the club, allowing free access to the harbour for lifting boats in and out or loading gear and offering support with laying moorings. Structural engineers WH MacKay of Fearn presented a trophy for the Moray Firth Cruiser race in 1983 and in 1985 the regatta was sponsored by Weldex, one of the first companies in the new industrial estate set up at Invergordon in the aftermath of the closure of the ill-fated aluminium smelter which had foundered in 1981 after only nine years production. Seaboard Anchors entered the scene in 1989, (and later Bilgewater Gin) sponsoring the Moray Firth Cruiser Race until the company was sold by Andy

Thoms to Gael Force in 1998. Gael Force have since offered financial support for younger sailors.

Although the club Dinghy Sailing training sessions in the 1980s were successful and well attended, few of those who graduated subsequently took up membership or racing and the dinghy section went into decline towards the end of the decade with racing being temporarily abandoned. Its fortunes were revived after Martyn Crawshaw gained RYA instructor qualifications in 1994 and, as a result of his enthusiasm, the section was revitalised and looking to expansion once more. Improvements to facilities continued in 1995 with the erection of a new storage shed for dinghies and other equipment with grant aid from the Scottish Sports Council, Ross and Cromarty Enterprise and the District Council, and in 1999 Dr Jackson submitted a successful application for funds from the National Lottery to buy a new rescue boat and other equipment.

There was no lack of other business to keep club officials off the streets at night. A helpful set of mooring guidelines was drawn up to assist members as a number of boats had broken free from moorings in the early years at Rosskeen. The Port Authority had offered assistance with laying and inspecting moorings but, eager to maintain its independence, the club declined this offer. Instead, Ron Stewart built a catamaran, appropriately named *Moorhen,* specifically for the purpose of laying and inspecting club members moorings. She was named after the class of government vessels known as Mooring Lighters used in naval dockyards for the laying and overhauling of moorings and operating boom defence nets with names such as *Moorhen, Moorfowl, Moorfire* and *Moorland.* Ron remembers these ships coming to the firth in the summer time to service the lines of naval mooring buoys stretching from the Yankee Pier to Cromarty. Ron, whose association with the club started in the late 1950s, was granted honorary membership of the club at the annual dinner dance in 1994 as a token of gratitude for his services in a variety of roles.

In 1985, after a long-running campaign extending over several years, the club was successful in having the Port Authority Bye Laws amended to allow certain exemptions for recreational craft.

The club acknowledged the invaluable support of Mr E Whelan of the RYA whose involvement had marked a turning point in negotiations with the Port Authority, but club commodores Douglas Young, Alistair Bulman and Ron Stewart also deserve recognition for their unstinting efforts in this long campaign.

But there were now other problems to contend with. A sewerage maceration scheme was proposed for Alness. The club argued for a full treatment plant instead with the support of the Highland River Purification Board but, although a good case was put forward, financial considerations dictated that only a maceration plant could be considered. The enormous volume of correspondence and effort put in to making the case largely fell to secretary Jean Cheyne who campaigned tirelessly on behalf of the club. Although this particular battle was lost there is still some hope as the RYA is now campaigning to have all recreational users included in the European Directive on Safe and Clean Waters rather than the current narrow reference to bathers.

Looking to the future development of the club, it was revealed early in 1983 that the Scottish Sports Council could only offer financial assistance to organisations with at least a 20 year lease on their property. The land on which the new clubhouse had been built was under a 35 year lease agreement with Highland Regional Council who, in turn, were tenants to farmer William Gill. The lease is due to expire in 2013 and, according to Scots Law, any building on the tenanted land would then belong to the landowner. Alternatively, on expiry of the lease, the clubhouse may have to be raised to the ground. It was therefore deemed to be in the interests of the club to seek to extend the lease or acquire the title to the land and so approaches were made to the council and Mr Gill to find a solution to this problem. This was very much a stop-start affair, the matter seemingly being forgotten about for some time then re-opened. Ten years passed and in 1993 it had still not been resolved and was raised once more. Six years later it was again on the agenda and in 2000 it was reported that the ground could not be purchased; Mr Gill would, however, be prepared to consider an extended lease but not the 99 year lease the club had sought. The sticky part of the problem is that it is the Highland Council which is the tenant, not Invergordon Boating Club, and with the lease due to expire in 2013, it is now a matter of urgency for the club to persuade the council to take action to protect the assets of the club.

The lessons of the past must not be forgotten; it took almost ten years to complete the arrangements for the flitting from the harbour to Rosskeen. The club would be wise to heed the proclamation of the Ross-shire Journal in 1928 '*the regatta is here to stay*'; unless this business is sorted out soon, it may not be here to stay at the present location.

Taking a longer term view, many members have expressed the hope that one day it may prove possible for the club to move back to the town. A base near the harbour, with berthing at pontoons, would be a vast improvement for boat owners compared with the present rather exposed site. It would make Invergordon a more attractive port for visiting yachts with potential economic benefits for businesses in the town and it may attract youngsters once more, for they are the club's lifeblood for the future.

In 1997 Jean Cheyne proposed marking the club's centenary year in some significant way. After some discussion it was agreed to stage an exhibition of memorabilia in Invergordon and produce a history of the club. A team of members began collecting information, pursuing research and interviewing people associated with the club in the past. This book is the result.

Working hard to win the Keel Wheel Trophy.

Chapter Seven

Characters and Comedies

A club may be defined as an association of people united by some common interest but the ethos of the club is shaped by the nature of individual members. Human character, as in a malt whisky or wine, takes some years to develop and may be the product of several influences, both human and environmental. It is always difficult to single out individuals for mention but some names shine brightly in the memories of many members and consistently are mentioned when yarns are told. These are some of the characters who may help to define the nature of Invergordon Boating Club in human terms.

Dougal Mackintosh

Many club members of the post-war period owed a debt of gratitude to Dougal Mackintosh, not only in respect of the number of rescues he carried out when boats overturned or were dis-masted, but also for his unfailing assistance in the arts of boatmanship. Christened Donald, but known universally as Dougal, he was born in 1896 and

lived in Clyde Street. On active service in the Dardanelles in the First World War, Dougal was also a boxing champion in the Royal Navy. Having served his apprenticeship aboard the coastal sailing vessel *Young Fox*, carrying coal home from Blyth, he later went deep-sea on tankers.

Elf.
Winner of the Duke of Sutherland's Cup, & Findhorn Cup.

In 1928, with business partners Willie Ross and Kenny Patience, he ran the Balblair to Invergordon Ferry until 1939 during which time he met his wife who travelled on the ferry each day to teach at Newhall School. The morning ferry was known as the school boat as scholars from the Black Isle within easy reach of the ferry found it more convenient to attend Invergordon Academy rather than travel by bus to Fortrose.

In the Second World War, he served on NAAFI vessels at Greenock and returned to run the ferry again after the war with the vessel *Modern Girl,* later taking up employment at the dockyard as skipper of the harbour launch until his retirement. This vessel also took pilots to and from ships using the firth and transported men and stores to the naval vessels at anchor.

Dougal part-owned and skippered *Elf* at one time. One of the most successful boats in the club from its early years until the 1950s, it changed hands several times and is now lying in derelict condition at Tomich Farm. He tutored generations of youngsters in the arts of rowing, bailing correctly, ie without scraping the bilge paint off as you bailed,

ropework, rigging, tidal conditions, navigational hazards and where to go and not to go in the various combinations of wind and tide likely to be encountered in the firth. Safety was of paramount importance and unfailingly he had a sharp word for any youngsters 'skylarking' about in boats. A cheerful character, he was always whistling and on one occasion when out in HAC Mackenzie's boat he asked HAC's young son James to point out the whistling buoy, a marker at the entrance to the firth which emitted a whistle. Young James pointed at Dougal himself and said, "You're the whistling boy. You're always whistling."

Dougal taught by example, always ensuring that the harbour launch was maintained to a high standard with brasses polished and decks and windows scrupulously clean, not always easy on a coal burner. The launch was secured at a pontoon at the end of the wooden section of the centre pier, now demolished, near where the lifeboat is now berthed. A workshop on this section served as a shore base for the launch and was choc-a-bloc with coils of rope, blocks, liferafts, candles, lamps, rowlocks, paddles, oars, heaving lines with monkey fists, grease and tallow; a veritable Aladdin's cave for youngsters who would be enthralled with his tales of life at sea.

Always deriving great pleasure in seeing youngsters mastering boating skills, Dougal maintained an interest in the club until his death in 1975.

Dougal Mackintosh.

Phil Durham

In the post-war years the club was very informal in its attitude and organisation. It was all about having good fun afloat. Phil Durham, club secretary at the time, recalls these days as some of the happiest of his life. Phil carried considerable authority in the club. Endowed with the respect due to a wartime submarine commander, he was the only member who knew how to work a slide rule (no calculators in these days) and so was responsible for handicapping. Phil had little time for Plymouth Yardstick numbers and complex calculations involving mast heights and sail areas. Not only an officer but also a gentleman, Phil cleverly devised his own handicapping system, which he swore by - and others swore at! A victim of polio, he would sit in his wheelchair studiously flicking the cursor on his slide rule to port or starboard, move the slide ahead or astern once or twice and then jot down some figures from his head against the name of each boat, carefully remembering who had won the previous week. Having run through all the fleet he would then announce the winner. The key to his system was that he intended to ensure that all the club members saw their names among the winners listed in the Ross-shire Journal. It would be dashed bad form to see the same few highly competitive members always collecting the prizes, and this way he kept them in check and spread the honours around so that, in a strange way, everyone was happy at some time. Primitive, loaded, effective, was how his sailing partner and brother-in-law Jim Paterson described Phil's system.

Phil remembers with mirth the day an elegant group of ladies were entertained by Colonel George Ross of Cromarty who invited them to enjoy an afternoon's racing aboard his yacht *Petunia*. Dressed in frilly frocks, the ladies sported themselves gracefully in the sun while Col Ross, with no regard for racing etiquette, boldly crossed the bows of several naval cutters eliciting some salty language from their crews. Disaster struck when one of the cutters ploughed into *Petunia* and stove in her side bringing the rigging down upon the hapless ladies. The boat was soon awash with the poor ladies in their frilly frocks up to their waists in chilly water, a source of great merriment

to the other crews. "That's what happens when soldiers go to sea", chuckled Phil, the ex-naval officer.

His physical disability did not deter Phil from sharing in adventures afloat and he managed to fit in a fair bit of sailing, usually crewing for Jim Paterson. In 1952, shortly before he was married, they were sailing back to Invergordon after competing at Cromarty in Jim's boat *Persephone*. Passing the ships of the Home Fleet, the light breeze suddenly freshened and *Persephone* was struck by a squall and capsized near an aircraft carrier. Jim and Phil clung to the capsized boat, expecting the carrier would send one of her boats to their assistance. Their plight went un-noticed. Eventually they managed to right her and lowered the sail, not an easy task with Phil having no mobility in his legs, and were busy bailing her out with the intention of sailing on when along came the reliable Dougal Mackintosh to the rescue in the ferryboat. Dougal took the hapless pair to the flagship, the battleship *HMS Vanguard*, before returning to the scene to tow the boat back to harbour. After checking that the pair were none the worse for their adventure they were returned to the harbour by one of *Vanguard's* boats.

The fact that their plight seemingly went unnoticed by the ships of the Home Fleet at anchor in the firth was a matter which incurred ex-naval officer Phil's severe displeasure; it was a dentist whose house overlooked the sea who had raised the alarm. On board *Vanguard* he asked for the name of the captain of the aircraft carrier whose watch-keeping had been defective and recognised it immediately as that of a former midshipman who had served under him. He promptly resumed his authority as a naval officer and sent his former subordinate a bollocking message about failing to maintain adequate watch.

Ironically, it had attracted the attention of a large number of spectators on Saltburn Road. While the drama was unfolding, Jim's mother and father were driving out to Cadboll to have tea at a cousin's house. Mrs Paterson was intrigued and enquired, "What do you think all these people are looking at Bill?" Mr Paterson was unimpressed and replied dismissively, "Huh. Nothing better to do with their time. Drive on dear, we'll be late for tea", blissfully

unaware that his son and future son-in-law were fighting for their lives in the chill waters of the firth.

Hugh Ross and Richard Brooke

Hugh Ross and Richard Brooke were the club's pioneers of west coast cruising and racing, regularly competing at Forth Week and the Oban and Clyde regattas in the post-war years. Hugh farmed at Lochslin by Fearn and carried on the family tradition, his father having also been a member and official of the club in its earlier years. An enthusiastic sailor who was instrumental in reviving the club after the war, Hugh sailed in *Ulva* which was built in 1903 as a thirty footer with a gunter rig. He converted her to a sloop and built a dog house for her. She was later sold to club members Ronnie and Sue Falconer from Balintore who careered into an oil rig in the North Sea while on passage to Norway. *Ulva* foundered but Sue and Ronnie were rescued. Undeterred by this mishap, they later set off on a round the world cruise on their next yacht, *Fleur d'Ecosse*.

Martin Legge, a veteran from the fifties, learned his sailing crewing for Hugh and Richard Brooke of

Cromarty Mains and recalled, "The only mechanical power on *Ulva* was a small, temperamental outboard engine, disrespectfully referred to by the skipper as 'Farting Fanny'. Coming through the canal, Hugh and Richard would lash their boats alongside a fishing boat to go through the locks but once out in Loch Ness, if the wind was favourable, they would race the fishing boats to the far end and were capable of beating them too. They were harum-scarum characters, right enough. On one occasion Hugh decided to take his boat up the Conon River with my brother Gordon on the foredeck swinging the lead and calling out the depth; they had no echo sounders in these days. They were so intent on keeping an eye on the depth of water that they failed to notice an overhead power cable. My brother had been holding on to the forestay and just let go to swing the lead when the mast struck the power line and brought it down. A second earlier and he would have been electrocuted."

Richard was a real enthusiast. He bought *Aerielle* in 1951 and later sold it to Ian Moodie of Evanton and then owned *Salotte* and *Sabrina*, a six metre class boat and one of the fastest ever built. They would sail down the east coast to the Forth to take part in regattas there, then through the Forth and Clyde Canal to the Clyde for more racing and on through the Crinan Canal to Oban to race there. After a spot of cruising they would return via the Caledonian Canal - and Richard never carried a chart on board. He knew the west coast like the back of his hand.

An ex Seaforth Highlander who had seen service in the Far East and the younger son of the late Sir Robert Brooke Bart DSO MC, Richard was also a member of the Royal Highland Yacht Club at Oban. He was tragically drowned in the Holy Loch in April 1958 aged only 36. He had been visiting his friend, Lt Col A J McAlpine whose motor yacht *Servabo,* a converted trawler, was lying at anchor off Sandbank. Both were keen yachtsmen and had been visiting the loch where *Sceptre,* the British challenger in the 1958 America's Cup Race, had recently been launched and was undergoing trials. The two men were returning to the yacht in a dinghy after a night ashore in the Oakbank Hotel when their dinghy overturned. The dinghy was found on the shore the next morning but the bodies of the two men were never recovered.

Close Encounters.

Launch of Faragon.

Liz Fraser	Ron Stewart
Commodore 1993-96	Commodore 1982-85

Shamrock.
Competed successfully at the Scottish Series,
West Highland Week and Moray Firth events.

Sabrina.
With Richard Brooke at the helm and
Hugh Ross on the stern.

Ulva.
Built in 1903 seen here with her gunter rig. Later changed
to a sloop rig when also fitted with a new doghouse.

Douglas Young

The coming of the smelter to Invergordon brought new members, new boats and new enthusiasm. Douglas Young was one such member who made a considerable contribution, not only to Invergordon Boating Club which he served at various times as secretary and commodore, but also to the North of Scotland sailing scene.

When Douglas arrived at the club it operated from an old shop with a leaky roof across the road from the old ferry slip. As a result of negotiations with McGruther and Marshall the club acquired land on either side of the slipway, a prudent move as the harbour was soon to expand and required the title to this land in a few years time. Douglas negotiated with his company to buy a disused hut left over from the construction of the smelter. It was erected on the new site, a secure compound was fenced off and the club now had reasonable premises adjacent to the harbour.

Membership flourished at this time and, with a more structured club, sailing became even more competitive. Douglas also introduced fun sailing events and picnic cruises across to the Black Isle.

But his most significant legacy must be the Moray Firth Cruiser Race which he introduced in 1973, now a firm favourite among the inter-club events in the Moray Firth area, and one in which Invergordon Boating Club members consistently excel.

At this time fish farms were becoming commonplace around the coast of Scotland and the Royal Yachting Association suggested the formation of a North of Scotland Yachting Association to provide local knowledge and assist with legal procedures to protect the interests of leisure sailors. Douglas was a founder member of the North of Scotland Yachting Association, serving as secretary and then chairman. Always an enthusiast, he produced a booklet of sailing directions for the various anchorages on the North East coast of Scotland. As chairman of the NSYA, Douglas enlisted the support of MPs and fought a hard battle on behalf of yachtsmen in the North to keep the crumbling Caledonian Canal from closure in 1977. His efforts were not in vain; many yachtsmen from the Moray Firth area, the rest of the UK and Europe now enjoy the benefits of the newly refurbished waterway as a route to and from the west coast which provides some of the best sailing in the world for yachtsmen.

His interest in sailing began in Freetown while working in Sierra Leone as an engineer; the British Governor had a GP14 dinghy and required a crew. Douglas brought *Zest* to Invergordon which he raced with Ron Stewart as crew, followed by *Sula* and then the beautiful 8 metre cruiser-racer, *Sonda,* the first of her class to be built. The Royal Northern and Clyde Yacht Club has a Sonda Room at Rhu, with a half model and photographs of all the 8 metre class boats built on the Clyde. These fine yachts race in the Annual Wooden Boat Regatta on the Clyde with *Sonda* winning seven out of the past nine races.

A skillful skipper, Douglas knew how to get the best from his boat and raced *Sonda* to one of the most remarkable finishes ever in the Moray Firth Cruiser Race. With Keith Stanley's trimaran *Boadicea* well ahead, a wind shift allowed *Sonda* to show her mettle and, sailing to windward, she overhauled the rest of the fleet and crept up on *Boadicea*. Both boats raced neck and neck for the finishing line, but *Boadicea's* early lead had proved just too great and she finished inches ahead of *Sonda*. At the reception after the race Douglas commented: "I can accept being beaten by another boat, but I hate being beaten by a contraption!"

Douglas Young. Comodore on three occasions.
A stalwart during the difficult years of change.
He brought fun and new ideas to the club.

Keith Stanley and Boadicea

Among the cruising fraternity on the west coast, the name of Keith Stanley is legendary; many have gained their yachtmaster's ticket under his tuition. Even better known is the famous trimaran he designed and built, *Boadicea.* Designed to meet his need for a safe family cruising boat, Keith decided to improvise on current trimaran designs in 1968 and build himself a fast boat which would allow his young family to play ashore during the day and when they were put to bed he would then set sail. With a boat capable of speeds up to about 15 knots it was possible to find another anchorage 30 to 50 miles away by sunset so that they would wake up to a new location each morning.

Built of ply with larch stringers on guarea frames and epoxy coated, she has featured in a number of publications, including Multihull International, as a significant development in trimaran design and she is still sailing from Little Loch Broom. Her speed is legendary. Having interrupted a cruise to attend a funeral in England, Keith met an old friend who remarked, "I hear you had a fast run down to Castlebay." The whole passage from Invergordon

to Barra had been completed in only 36 hours. "How on earth do you know?" Keith asked. "I was speaking to a fishing boat skipper in Stornoway. You were the talk of the fishing fleet. They were all calling each other up on the radio to watch out for you as you went flying down the Minch."

Boadicea started as a cruising boat. With a 19 foot beam, she is not really suitable for racing round the cans but as a cruiser-racer she was a formidable adversary. In her first entry in the Moray Firth Cruiser Race in 1976 she was so far ahead of the field at the finishing line at Cromarty that she carried on to Invergordon where the crew all showered and then drove by car round to the hotel at Cromarty to join the race party. They arrived just as Dan Boddington's *Dolphin of Rhu*, the second boat over the line and also of IBC, was dropping anchor. Over an hour separated the first two boats home. Even more startling was the fact that Keith, being a newcomer to the area and having been invited to take part in the race, had actually gone on a wrong course near the start and covered an extra two miles! Under the circumstances he did the gentlemanly thing and formally retired from the race allowing Dan, who had invited him to take part, to take home the trophy.

In the years to follow she earned a considerable reputation in the north racing circuit but her racing days were numbered when she was driven ashore by the tail end of a hurricane which hit the Scottish coast in the late 1970s. Anchored off Isle Martin at the entrance to Loch Broom with a storm imminent, Keith had two bower anchors set. After some time it seemed as if the wind was beginning to abate and he went ashore to phone home from a telephone box. Standing in the phone box, he noticed an ominous looking black curtain sweep in from the sea, obliterating each island and headland in its path. He could see what looked like confetti whirling around in the wind - the wreckage of caravans, pieces of roofing and wooden sheds. This was major trouble. He left the phone box and rushed back to the beach to launch his dinghy. Dragging it into the water the squall struck with colossal force. The dinghy was ripped from his grasp and sucked up in the air, still with outboard engine attached, and was carried off with the rest of the wreckage. A clinker built rowing boat on the beach was lifted and tossed on to some rocks where it smashed open like a barrel. With no means left to get back on board *Boadicea* which was now dragging both anchors, he asked a fish farm lad to take him out. "You must be mad", was the perfectly reasonable reply. But Keith was not in a perfectly reasonable mood. "If you don't take me, I'll swim out", was his reply. The lad took him out in a dory and, as they ran alongside *Boadicea,* Keith grabbed at a shroud and hauled himself aboard. There was nothing he could do. The anchor ropes were locked tight. The vessel was slowly dragging backwards. The two anchors, ploughing the bottom, slowly began to converge. He looked back at the dory. She could make no headway against wind and was blown on to the beach; the lad jumped as she reared on the surf and managed to drag himself ashore. The dory was lifted off the surf by the wind and blown over and over right up the beach. Inevitably, *Boadicea* was also pushed back on to the shore. In the pounding surf, her outriggers were smashed. Keith jumped ashore and ran off to borrow a tractor. Back on the beach, he managed to get a line aboard and hauled her out of the punishing waves, a sorry sight, but with the main hull apparently still intact.

The insurance surveyor was amazed. He had surveyed the boat ten years earlier when she had been built. Apart from the two outriggers which would have to be rebuilt, the main hull was as solid as the day she had been launched suffering only superficial damage. It took two years to repair her. Meanwhile, the aluminium smelter where Keith worked closed and he set himself up in business as a sailing school with the monohull, *Piota*.

On his last voyage in the newly repaired *Boadicea* he introduced Jan, an attractive girl from Dundee, to Topher, a civil engineer from the west coast as his crew for the trip. A year later they were married. Some time later they bought *Boadicea* and now, with a young family aboard her once again, the 33 year old trimaran has reverted to being a family cruiser once more.

Many people owe much to Keith for his instruction. A hard sailing master, he teaches crew how to make the most of the sailing experience, be it calm or blowing a gale. Few days are lost due to the weather; sailing overnight allows time to explore islands during the daytime and gives valuable nightime experience to crews. Peter and Jean Cheyne recalled a once-in-a-lifetime experience on a trip to St Kilda with Keith on *Piota* while Peter was undertaking his Coastal Skipper's practical course. Heading out from the Sound of Harris, they arrived at the archipelago at midnight sailing round Boreray in clear moonlight with the Northern Lights flickering upwards into the sky. Stac an Armin and Stac Lee were eerie black hulks looming darkly out of a silver sea, their black precipitous sides peppered with the white forms of thousands of fulmars resting for the night. This was an experience which could never have been matched by viewing the same islands in daylight.

The Murray Dynasty

Duncan Murray is renowned in Scottish yachting circles as an aggressive and very successful competitor. His association with the club stretches back to the 1950s when, as a boy, he crewed for an equally aggressive competitor, Ian Moodie, in *Aerielle,* the 6 metre class boat previously owned by Richard Brooke.

Inspired by Ian's single-mindedness, it proved to be an effective apprenticeship. Duncan has won just about every trophy available in the North Sailing circuit and a few more in the Clyde and West Highlands, having been introduced to the highly competitive west coast racing scene by Ian in 1958. Duncan always goes to sea with one objective - to win.

After initially crewing on keelboats, the first real boat he owned was a dinghy. He then graduated back up the scale owning a succession of fast keelboats; *Redskin, Starlet* and *Sagacious* have gathered silverware like barges gather barnacles with a total of six North of Scotland Championship wins between them.

Duncan correctly points out that whatever success his boats have had has been due to having a highly competent crew cast in the same mould; they function as a team and want to win. Over the years he has attracted a succession of young men who have grown up in the club; boys like Terry Macleod, Mark Robson and his two sons Andrew and Colin, all excellent sailors with individual track records of success allowing Duncan to sit back and enjoy the scene now while they make the decisions and do all the work.

Duncan has served the club as Secretary and Commodore but perhaps his lasting legacy to the club has been his influence in improving racing. Since taking over the organisation of the Moray Firth Cruiser Race initiated by Douglas Young, Duncan developed the race from a one class race to two and later three classes, attracting ever more entries and firmly establishing it as the most popular race in the North of Scotland.

His determination to see good racing technique in the club led to the introduction of cruisers racing round the very tight dinghy courses, which sharpened the skills of skippers and crews and has no doubt honed the competitiveness of Invergordon Boating Club members with results evident in the range of trophies gathered by members at various regattas.

Duncan also set the competitive edge with his own expertise and, with his strong young crew, he is capable of competing anywhere with success. He is equally expert on the use of the Rule Book and has often put members on edge with his enthusiasm for the Protest System. On one occasion it backfired on him. Andy Thoms in *Pendragon* had gone aground three times during one race and Duncan argued that he should be protested out for "unseamanship behaviour". Andy replied dismissively, "Unseamanship behaviour? Even after going aground three times I still had the beating of you!"

Duncan's two sons are following in his wake. Andrew was the youngest ever winner of the Moray Firth Cruiser Race and Colin has established an outstanding reputation on the national yachting scene. Joining the Royal Marines after leaving school, Colin quickly established himself as one of their leading yachtsmen winning a host of championships throughout the 1990s. Four times winner of the British Peaks Race, three times winner of the Scottish Peaks Race and twice winner of the British Match Racing Championship, in 1998 he won Scottish Series Championship at Tarbert in a fleet of over 300 boats, the British Solling Championship, winning at every regatta in which he competed, and then took fourth place in

the European Championships. In 1999 he continued to excel, adding the Scottish and British Solling titles, the Fastnet Race, the European Services Championship and took second place in the World Services Championships at Keil. He was also a member of the Commonwealth Team which won the Pre-Admiral's Cup Race at Cowes in the 50 footer *Chernikeef* and the team went on to gain fourth place in the Admiral's Cup. He is currently in training as a member of the crew for the next America's Cup and reached the final selection trials for the British Olympic team in 2000.

These are merely a selection of Colin's achievements. He has competed with distinction throughout the world and claims his success was founded on his early crewing days at Invergordon, particularly under the watchful eye of skipper Billy MacFarlane who instilled in him the attitude that you always give 100% in every race. Colin is now a high performance manager for the Royal Yachting Association, recruiting and training coaches and bringing on young sailors with future olympic potential. He can clearly claim to be the most successful racing sailor ever produced by the Invergordon Boating Club.

*Left: Teenager
Duncan Murray.*
The catalyst which has
stimulated such competative
sailing at Invergordon
Boating Club.

*Below: Colin Murray
and Terry MacLeod.*

Ron Stewart.
Being presented with Honorary Membership,
11th November 1994.

Ron Stewart

Ron is one of the longest serving members of the club having been introduced to sailing in the 1950s when he, Duncan Murray and Dennis Mellon as schoolboys, took a great interest in the harbour. These boys were always on hand to offer their services as crew to club stalwarts Hugh Ross, Richard Brooke, HAC MacKenzie and Ian Moodie who gave the boys a good grounding in seamanship. These informal arrangements bred enthusiastic sailors; nowadays the club has to have a Child Protection Policy without which it would be ineligible for any grant assistance. A modest and unassuming character, Ron has served the club with distinction over almost five decades. He is a fund of knowledge regarding boats and boating and is forever attending quietly to maintenance jobs, moorings and slipway care and, following the example of his mentors, Ron is always willing to offer help and advice to new members - a real gentleman sailor. Elected Club Commodore in 1982, an office he held for three years, Ron's sterling service to the club was recognised by the conferring of honorary membership in 1994.

Liz Fraser

Liz has the distinction of being the club's first female Commodore, serving from 1993 to 1996.

In the Chauvinistic Edwardian era when the club was founded ladies were not allowed to vote. Fifty years later in the rapidly changing society of the post-war period female members were allowed full membership and began to take on official roles in the sixties; but it took almost another thirty years before the male dominated membership elected a female to highest office in the club.

Liz breezed in as Commodore in October 1993 like a breath of fresh air, her style, individuality and artistic flair bringing new life to the club. She had a benign moderating influence on aggressive male tendencies. During her period of office, dinghy sailing was revived under the enthusiastic training of Martyn Crawshaw. Liz gave her full support to this revival and, with the help of Ron Christie from the Outdoor Education Department, she was able to hire a small fleet of Topper dinghies for the season - ideal boats for youngsters to learn sailing. But this growth resulted in a need for more storage space for dinghies and gear and some of the men folk expressed imperialist desires to colonise the ladies changing room for this purpose. Liz, being of a generous nature, announced that she would have no objection to sharing the men's changing room. Chauvinism was stunned into silence. The ladies still have their own changing room. It would be only fair to record that other ladies were less enthusiastic about sharing changing facilities with the men and so Liz embarked on a bid to obtain a new storage shed which is now greatly appreciated by members over the summer months and provides cover for the club dinghies during the winter.

Being a Home Economics teacher, feeding at regatta times was at its height and Liz also introduced a fun evening of nautical nonsense and quiz games. She also brought style and a sense of humour to suit every occasion. When Ron Stewart was building his catamaran *Faragon* in his garage, he would leave a message on the blackboard in the clubhouse galley for helpers to move a hull or some other task requiring extra muscle and, after a night's racing a band of willing helpers would arrive at Barbaraville to offer assistance. The same band of helpers attended the launching ceremony, carrying hulls and assembling the vessel prior to the launch. Liz, as Commodore, was invited to perform the naming ceremony and arrived in the afternoon in her nautical uniform - navy blue culottes, matching nautical jacket with brass buttons and epaulettes and her Venetian Gondolier's hat. Only one thing was missing - the piper. Andy Thoms had forgotten but hastily got himself to Barbaraville and waded into the sea playing his pipes as Ron and Liz boarded the vessel. The naming ceremony was graciously performed with flags flying and Liz was given the opportunity to inspect the vessel. To the amazement of the onlookers she and Ron disappeared below for some considerable time. Eventually Ron re-appeared alone and rowed ashore. It took some time before the onlookers realised that Ron had abandoned Liz onboard and, dressed in all her nautical finery, she couldn't get ashore. Andy, like a true Highland Gentleman hastily threw down his pipes, waded out to a depth above his waist and offered Liz a piggy-back ashore which she was only too pleased to accept with good humour.

Chapter Eight
All At Sea

Watching a yacht manoeuvre under sail in the control of a competent skipper belies the skill and years of hard-won experience of the skipper and crew. Such occurrences bring quiet pleasure and satisfaction but all experienced sailors were novices at one time. Then the learning curve is steep and often painful - and the memories linger.

In the 1970s Peter Cheyne and George Shields entered a joint venture to purchase a sailing boat, a fine little Hurley 18 called *Zephyr*. Her hull was so beautifully smooth and shiny with an encapsulated keel that Peter and George decided no weed could ever take hold on such a silken surface, so why bother with expensive anti-fouling? That was their first mistake. In anticipation of future launches and recoveries, George had wisely invested in a pair of green, waist-high waders. High tide arrived in the evening as, in failing light, the trailer was backed down the slipway for the first launch. Clad in his waders, George was the guide with Peter driving. Unfortunately, the trailer veered off-centre on the

slip and George, intent on trying to see the wheels through the water, stepped backwards off the slip into neck-high water. A harsh lesson was learned on the hydrodynamic properties of a pair of thigh waders filled with water and the general reluctance of colleagues to come to one's assistance in freezing cold water.

Peter had come new to sailing and George had had some dinghy sailing experience but their combined experience of racing was nil. Undeterred by this, they set off to compete in the Chanonry Sailing Club Regatta. Official handicaps at this point remained a mystery to the merry mariners whose limited ability to get the boat to point in the desired direction had proved handicap enough, enabling them to claim the longest recorded passage time from Invergordon to Fortrose of six hours. When the Officer of the Day called out a request for their PY number, Peter looked blankly at George and whispered nervously, "What on earth is a PY Number?" George looked blankly back at Peter. The OOD had as much chance of an answer had he asked for their National Insurance Number. Still undaunted, the bold boys set off with the rest of the fleet, starting creditably near the front and ahead of many bigger boats. Things were looking up indeed. After a while they were puzzled that the rest of the fleet were sailing in a strange direction. With the supreme confidence borne of naivety, they pushed on regardless round the East Riff Buoy which, due to a slight error in chart work, they had mistaken for the West Riff Buoy, and, heading back to Fortrose in a commanding position, they blythely discussed who should go up to collect the trophy while the rest of the fleet carried on round the proper course for the day. This partnership, while very amicable, did suffer some strain in its early days. A dairy farmer, Peter saw no need to buy expensive yachtie wellies when he could use the same boots he wore when mucking out the byre much to George's dismay.

Most aspiring sailors do the sensible thing and learn the ropes by crewing on someone else's boat. An observant crew can often save the skipper from disaster, or at least extreme embarrassment. Though the Cromarty Firth is noted for its deep waters there are shallows on either side which extend far out to sea, presenting a hidden hazard for the unobservant skipper.

In his early sailing days, George Shields remembers coasting along the Udale Bay side of the firth with his wife and young daughter, Lesley, as crew. Unimpressed by the technicalities of sailing, Lesley frequently had to be rebuked by her mother for hanging over the side of the boat and looking into the sea, but her timely cry of, "Look at the crabs, Mum", spared the skipper from humiliation. Although still half a mile offshore, they were sailing in only three feet of water. He hurriedly tacked out of danger.

It was a pity Peter didn't have her aboard some years later when, by now an experienced racing skipper, he was surging home to almost certain victory in a NSYA 7 Series race at Chanonry. Carried away by the fine sight of *Egret* thrusting along in full sail, foam frothing along her lee rail, Peter looked behind in smug satisfaction at the rest of the fleet in his wake and proudly imagined another trophy sitting on his sideboard. Then his eye caught the figures flickering on the sounder. *Egret* was in extremely shallow water. In a panic, he ordered a change of tack. The crew responded immediately. The boat swung round, sat upright in the water and her keel ploughed into the sand, wedging itself firmly on the bottom. Nothing would mover her to the delight of the rest of the fleet as they surged past towards the finishing line waving cheerily. As Peter and his hapless crew sat disconsolately on the Skate Bank waiting for the tide to rise, the Chanonry Sailing Club generously ferried out plates of mince and tatties to sustain them in their misery.

But Peter wasn't always such an reckless sailor. Racing in a 7 series race in 1982 in *Athene,* he was scolded by his sixteen year old daughter Kirsty for being too cautious. It had been agreed that he would take the tiller on the windward legs and she would take the downwind legs. With Kirsty at the helm and a bulging spinnaker aloft, *Athene* was flying before the wind. But Peter became more than a little agitated as her speed increased until the log registered 10 knots. He may have relinquished the helm, but it was still his boat and he decided to assert his authority. He fidgeted, twitched, looked up at the pregnant sail, looked down at the bows dipping deeper into the water, breathed in heavily and stammered, "Eh, hrumm, eh, 10 knots..." When this elicited no response from the helm, panic set in

and he stood up and blurted out authoritatively, "Time to get the spinnaker down". The young helmswoman was singularly unimpressed by her crew's intervention and retorted dismissively, "Oh sit down Dad and be quiet, I'm concentrating!"

Other young female sailors have shown that they are a force to be reckoned with though they may not always be as single-minded as their male counterparts. Julie Mardon and Catriona Campbell in their excellent Nigg Cup win in 1985 were unsure where the finishing line actually was and carried on past Cromarty towards Nigg and then on between the Sutors until eventually, in a sizeable swell, only the masthead could be seen above the wave crests. With dolphins playing around their boat they were delighted to carry on and would happily have sailed on to Nairn if the dolphins had stayed with them. Eventually, the rescue boat shepherded them back to Cromarty where Duncan Murray on *Even Up* had to endure the embarrassment of having lost an anchor. *Even Up* appeared to have missed the harbour entrance.

Without power, the outboard bracket having broken off the transom, he was heading for the rocks when

Mark Robson threw out the anchor and uncharacteristically forgot to secure the warp on deck! They managed to get in safely but, on complaining that the rescue boat had ignored their pleas for help in rushing off to turn Julie and Catriona around, they were bluntly told that they were old enough to look after themselves.

The dolphins also proved an exciting diversion for Karaine Harnetty who, as a plucky nine-year old, set off in the Nigg Cup race single-handed, her father keeping a close watch on her progress from the rescue boat. For company, on the floor of her Mirror dinghy, *Reflections,* Karaine had a portable radio with her. The music seemed to excite the dolphins. Much to Karaine's delight, they suddenly appeared beside her jumping and diving all round her dinghy which began to rock like mad. Her agitated father rushed over in the rescue boat and roared at her to "Turn that radio off!" Karaine is still devoted to the sea and regularly goes early morning fishing off Rockfield. It is not known if she still uses the radio to attract the fish.

Schoolteacher Andy Murray confesses that the skipper's report on one of his first voyages might have read, 'Could have done better'. Attempting to climb aboard Charlie Murdoch's fine old ketch *Marie Louise* at Nigg, he stepped out over the choppy waters between the pier and the pitching deck and grabbed a rope dangling from the pier only to discover it was not secured. He was picked up, literally, from the sea by the crew. Drying off down below, it was clear that the crew had been enticed aboard by the promise of liberal quantities of liquid refreshment. They were bound for Findhorn for the start of an overnight race to Lybster and the blustery conditions were ideal for *Marie Louise*. Not that it did them any good, for the priority on the way over was to get a good meal inside the crew and they arrived an hour late for the start. Underway at last, Andy felt honoured to be asked to take the helm of this grand old lady of the IBC fleet. As the evening wore on it became clear that he was the only one capable of doing the job; the rest having dozed off down below after enjoying the skipper's generous hospitality. Charlie's navigation instructions were simple.

"Keep that star just to the left of the big mast."
"What do I do if it gets cloudy?" asked Andy.

"Switch on the penlight torch sellotaped to the mizzen mast and shine it on the compass, but don't leave it on for long, the batteries are about done". And with that he retired below, leaving Andy to find Lybster. He did. At least he found the harbour bottom and stuck fast. The other boats, having arrived long before *Marie Louise,* were all darkened for the night and with the rest of the crew sound asleep he decided to join them below. Awakening to the sizzling of bacon he became aware that the vessel was lying at an angle of 45 degrees much to everyone else's hilarity and Charlie's deep embarrassment.

Sailing is full of surprises. There have been many occasions when football matches on public parks have been interrupted by the intervention of an enthusiastic dog intent on having some of the action, but the same thing happened about thirty years ago at the start of an IBC race. David Lipp, who also did some shooting for wildfowl at the time, left his faithful and obedient spaniel, Nick, on the slip while he set off in his dinghy to jostle for position prior to the start of the race. As expected of a well-trained gun dog, Nick sat dutifully by the water's edge until the report of the starting gun signalled, in his doggy mind, that a duck must have come down in the firth. He knew what was expected of him and immediately plunged into the water and paddled around determinedly among the boats looking for a dead bird until he was eventually hauled aboard Dave's boat. Dave did not win the race that day.

Gerald Landale, the owner of *Roxby,* a lug-sailed Shetland sixern, is a dyed-in-the-wool traditional boat enthusiast who thrives on the smell of tar, wood and varnish. He is a regular participant in the Portsoy Traditional Boat Festival, a magnet for boat lovers, tourists and curious spectators. Having some work on the rigging to do he decided to spend some slack time at the festival on his ropework. Just as he started the rain came on, and gathering his coils of rope, hard eyes and splicing tools he sought shelter in a waterfront doorway while he did his work. Almost unaware of the crowd of onlookers which quickly assembled to watch his nimble fingers deftly splice rope in this ancient mariner's craft, he was rather taken aback when he finished to a round of applause. Surprised at his

Ku-Mara.
A constant winner and Club Champion
for the past two years.

Roxby.
Winner in her class at the Port Day Traditional Boat Festival.

Sonda.
Doug. Young's
pride and joy.

Boadicea.
A unique and most splendid trimaran designed and built by
Keith Stanley.

unwitting entertainment potential, he was even more surprised on learning of his earning potential when one of the appreciative onlookers then said, "That was most interesting, but where do we pay for your demonstration?"

George O'hara's boat *Coffee Cream* was the first club boat to compete in the annual Banff-Stavanger Race. Although an experienced sailor, it was his first blue water race and with no previous such experience to call on the watch word as always was PREPARATION, PREPARATION, PREPARATION. Planning meetings were held with full crew and wives to assign tasks. The wives sorted out the eating arrangements and provisioning with masterly detail. Food was prepared and labelled with an overall eating plan detailing what was for each day and where it would be stored, with main courses such as lamb casserole & veg bake, beef casserole with potatoes, lasagne & veg in cheese sauce, bacon, eggs, tomatoes and mushrooms. Every taste was catered for; no one would go hungry on this voyage. At the reception dinner at Banff on the eve of the race George and his crew shared a table with a Norwegian crew who had

spent three whole weekends preparing sandwiches for the two-way trip. The Scots said nothing but felt rather superior at the thought of the gastronomic delights they would enjoy while the Norwegians would only have cold sandwiches. But pride comes before a fall. The weather turned so bad that the violent movement of the boat prevented them from even making a cup of coffee. When one of the crew tried he ended up with scalding water all over him and next to nothing in the mug. For two and a half days meals consisted of breaking lumps off a large fruit cake and washing it down with bottled water. The skipper, in a fit of adventure, decided to make himself some weetabix in milk. This took about 15 minutes to do, as between each ingredient being found, the plate had to be wedged into a suitable crevice. When it was eventually all prepared and the ingredients had all been re-stored a pitiful voice from one of the bunks said, " Is that weetabix you're making? Could you make some for me?" "$% *@! *!!", came the skipper's muttered reply between clenched teeth. The watch system suffered a similar fate. Possible systems are two hour, three hour static, four hour rotating, two person, three person combinations, overlapping five person system and iolaire system. After lengthy debates and a study of watch systems tried on round the world races, they decided on a combination of two systems. Because there were five of a crew this was an overlapping two hour on - two hour off rota with one hour only on the midnight watch as this was likely to be the most taxing. It also meant cooking duties would be shared throughout the crew. Technology was brought in to simplify things and a schedule was drawn up on the computer with colour coding for each person so that it was possible to see at a glance who was on and allowed for the worst scenario of taking five days for the crossing. The whole thing took about three hours to compile plus discussion time. Only six hours into the race the fancy colour-coded watch-keeping schedule was rendered useless; one crew member took really ill with seasickness and was confined to bed for the duration of the trip. With four left it was decided to work in two teams on a two hour on, two hour off rota. This, of course, took only about five seconds to work out. With following strong winds

the boat made Stavanger in very good time. Only three were returning on the boat so it was decided to make the shortest crossing, from Bergen to Shetland, in case of bad weather. Following an interesting and leisurely three day cruise up the fiords to Bergen, *Coffee Cream* turned westwards to Shetland in flat calm weather. Halfway across, with the good weather continuing, she changed course and made straight for Orkney. Half way there, she turned again for Wick and then followed the coast back to Invergordon. The trip took 62 hours under engine in a flat calm with the autohelm looking after the steering. As the crew sat on deck in the middle of the North Sea at 11 pm, basking in the mellow light of a glorious sunset mirrored on a silken sea, a large Drambuie in one hand and a hot, baked King Edward in the other it was easy to forget the troubles encountered on the outward route; cold and damp, sleep deprivation, seas like tenement buildings, surfing down the waves at speeds the boat shouldn't be doing. In this euphoric state what else could they do but make plans for the next adventure; all of which would, of course, require meticulous PREPARATION!

Chapter Nine

Salty Talk

It is no doubt best that youngsters of both sexes are introduced to the arts of sailing and its speculiar language at an early age. Many wives have come rather later to sailing, often press-ganged into crewing for enthusiastic husbands, and they not infrequently fall into the trap of using everyday language with unintentional ambiguity.

The first major cruise planned by the Shields family was to venture through the Caledonian Canal to the West Coast. On the eve of the departure, George, assisted by co-owner Peter, sailed the boat round to the canal. *Zephyr* was equipped with a small outboard engine which had no reverse gear - to go astern meant rotating the engine through 180 degrees. On their arrival at the canal entrance, the wind was blowing strongly from the west, straight into the canal sea lock. Experienced skippers would have stood off till the lock gates opened, but not our pair; in they went with the wind on their tails hurrying them along at increasing speed. George tried to counter the force of the wind by rotating the engine to provide reverse thrust. It stalled - and refused to start. The wind drove them forward towards the massive lock gates. Fortunately, the lock-keeper had already started to open the gates and cleared just enough space for the boat to surge through with only inches to spare. Re-united with their wives Moira and Jean at Muirtown basin, they decided to use the towpath for its original purpose and tow the boat through the locks. Although there was no horse available the ladies provided a suitable substitute, though they wouldn't take the bit between their teeth. A couple of long ropes were produced with Moira controlling the stern line. She too appeared to be having problems with wind when, in front of a gathering crowd of onlookers, she dutifully called out to her skipper, "Just let me know when to let off!" George is no less guilty of falling prey to the double entendre. Looking out of his window at Balintore one day with a full gale blowing, he saw a yacht loom out of the clouds of spindrift blowing across the bay. Its mainsail appeared to be coming adrift and when he saw the sail come down he became concerned that the vessel was in difficulty.

Of course, he did the right thing and contacted the coastguard immediately. Unknown to George, it was his highly experienced fellow club member Keith Stanley who thought little of sailing in such conditions in his trimaran *Boadicea*. George was correct in his assumption that there had been a problem; a monohulled boat would heel to the pressure of the wind but such was the force of the wind on the relatively unyielding trimaran that the nylon sail slides were popping out of the mast track, their wings having been sheared off by the forces at play. However, this was a relatively minor problem to Keith who had hove-to and begun to remove slides from the foot of the sail and transfer them to the luff - all part of the day's work. A few minutes later *Boadicea* was beating into the wind again bound for Invergordon. Then a search and rescue helicopter appeared overhead; it had a quick look and moved off to search round the firth. Finding no other vessel at sea that day it returned for another look, and hovered overhead. The helicopter winchman waved at Keith. Keith happily waved back. Then the Invergordon lifeboat appeared out from the sutors and headed towards *Boadicea*. At this point Keith began to have a sinking feeling in his stomach. He went below, switched on the radio and called the coastguard. Sure enough, they were out looking for him and to make matters worse, it was lifeboat 2nd cox Sandy MacKenzie, also an IBC member, at the helm of the lifeboat. Just to underline the fact that *Boadicea* was in no trouble at all, as the lifeboat bore round alongside them Keith mischievously tightened his sheets. *Boadicea,* cutting through the waves at a good 10 knots, surged ahead of the lifeboat, an old Watson which could at best make 8 knots. The gap between yacht and lifeboat increased and the crew of *Boadicea* waved gleefully at the lifeboat struggling in their wake as they surged through the Sutors and into the Cromarty Firth. On learning that it was George who had raised the alarm, Keith decided to have more sport and rang him up to give him a mock bollocking. Poor George was so embarrassed and blurted out his apologies finishing with the remark, "If I had known it was you, I would never have bothered to call out the rescue services." Keith is still not sure which meaning to take from that.

Andy Thoms remembers his aunt Marjorie, a noted figure in the Clyde racing scene and winner of the Royal Clyde Centenary Trophy in 1955, coming to race in the Cromarty Firth with John Scott of Fearn. Out of deference, John had given the helm to his distinguished guest. She was going well but was being increasingly forced on to a lee shore by another yacht outside her, both on the port tack. When she could see the bottom, she decided it was time to tack out but was prevented from doing so by the close proximity of the other yacht. In best Clyde fashion, she called out in a stentorian voice, "Water please!" John then remarked in a quietly conversational voice, "Ach, it's no use asking him for water, Marjorie, he'll only think you want it for your whisky".

But the centenary prize for the most entertaining ambiguity of all must go to Liz Fraser. Liz, the club's first lady Commodore, has endured numerous moments of terror while crewing for husband Fred but none more so than when, in a thrilling race with a blustery following wind, she had to grapple on a heaving foredeck with a delinquent spinnaker apparently intent on dragging her overboard. Like the competent crew she was, after all such a distinguished figure as the Club Commodore could never be seen losing face with a recalcitrant spinnaker, she managed with great difficulty to get the wayward sail stowed and then turned to vent her spleen on her skipper. She may have been crew but she held the rank of Commodore - and more powerful even than that - she was his wife! Her voice could be heard throughout the fleet which convulsed in laughter as she roared aft, "Fred Fraser, if you stick that thing up again we'll be sleeping in separate beds!" Later, in the clubhouse, she added the postscript: "And I meant every word!"

Perhaps the experienced Charlie Murdoch got it right. Going up the locks at Muirtown with Peter Cheyne, Charlie became fascinated with a beautiful girl crewing on a French yacht also going up the locks. After a period of time feasting his eye on this delightful distraction, Charlie turned to Peter and remarked, "She can't possibly be the skipper's wife". "Why not?" asked Peter. "She's far too friendly", came the reply, obviously borne of experience.

Chapter Ten

From Humble Beginnings

Some sage once claimed that owning a boat was like standing in a cold shower tearing up pound notes. Ian Forbes, having just bought *Ketchup,* a Hunter Europa, was inclined to agree and suggested that boat ownership was a bit like keeping another woman. Donnie MacDonald disagreed. He said it was better!

Certainly until the middle of the 20th century the cost of yachting ensured that it remained an activity for only those with adequate leisure time and disposable income. However, after the Second World War it became within reach of the ordinary working man with a limited budget. And now, although enthusiasts will still lavish love and care and money on their beloved craft, it is possible to make your way into the sport from very humble beginnings. Indeed it has never been easier to get yourself afloat.

In the post-war years with so many ships being broken up it was possible for lifeboats to be purchased for a few pounds. Airborne lifeboats too

were being sold off. Designed by Uffa Fox, these excellent double-skinned mahogany boats were capable of being converted into sailing or motor boats with a little work and ingenuity and it was from such humble beginnings that some IBC members were able to experience their first command.

Dick Ross and Don Hendry acquired an airborne lifeboat from a Coastal Command airfield in Morayshire and rigged it for sailing. Surplus to requirements, it cost the princely sum of £15 and they managed to secure a second boat for an additional £8. Both boats were beached at Balintraid pier and work commenced on fitting out. Francis Ross of Invergordon made a rudder, a masterpiece of carpentry, and other dockyard mateys provided help and advice. A mast and rigging of a design approved for the class of boat was obtained and they named their boat *Highflyer* after the RN depot in Trincomalee where they had both been stationed and had such happy memories in what was then Ceylon. The second boat was sold to cover their expenses. With their improvised boat both men enjoyed exhilarating racing for a number of years until relinquishing their status as skippers for the subordinate role as husbands in matrimony.

Others started from even more humble and crude beginnings. Martin Legge and Duncan Murray recall sailing about in the firth in converted aircraft fuel tanks. With no thought for their own safety they never considered the need for life jackets until Gilbert Ross the ironmonger sold some old flying suits for two shillings and sixpence. These were filled with Kapok and cut off at the waist where bindings were stitched for tying round the waist. In these more relaxed times boys were were always to be found around the harbour and provided crews for club members who owned real boats.

After the removal of the club premises to Rosskeen, this steady supply of young blood all but dried up. Mark Robson and Terry MacLeod were the last of the young lads who came to the club on their own initiative. Cycling out from Invergordon they made the best use of the facilities available to them. They initially learned to sail by crewing with Ron Stewart, who was one of a generation of boys always hanging around the harbour back in the 1950s and had himself been similarly encouraged

by Hugh Ross. Joining the dinghy sailing classes, they were so enthusiastic and soon became very proficient sailors. Their summer holidays were spent out in the dinghies causing the club some consternation over their safety. This was before health and safety regulations began to bite and the club committee, not wishing to curtail their enthusiasm, wrote to their parents asking them to accept full responsibility for the boys' safety. There was no stopping them and, as regular crew members with Duncan Murray and his son Andrew, these two have gone on to achieve significant success. Terry and Andrew are also members of the crew of Invergordon Lifeboat.

David Vass's story is perhaps typical of the development of many sailors around Scottish coasts. Brought up in Balintore it was imperative that David had to have a boat. While staying with his grandparents in Tain he purloined the packing cases of an aunt who had arrived from Canada and built his first boat, a heavy slab-sided flat-bottomed punt. It leaked like a sieve, could transport one, or with great care, occasionally two boys across the seven metre width of the river at Tain. A succession of craft later followed from the Vass yard as technical skills increased. The punt shape gave way to multi-chine. Packingbox plywood was overtaken by more exotic, but still free materials like lath frame covered with polythene or tractor inner tube lashed to a wooden frame. Some of these craft could cope with six inch waves and one, the polythene skinned canoe could even take a single lobster creel to sea. His uncle, A V MacLeod later bought an 18 foot catamaran, a real sailing boat at last and what a flyer. It hummed and growled like a living creature as the wind played in the rigging and the twin hulls sliced through the sea. The magical motive power of the wind was addictive and captivated him. He was hooked. Then his father acquired a decrepit clinker built rowing boat. After a lot of work she was ready for the sea. It was his first command.

As is the way of things, after a couple of years its limited range was inhibiting. Reading sailing books and magazines whetted his appetite for more adventurous sailing. Now he wanted a cruising boat. A lifeboat from a former accommodation ship when the yard was being built at Nigg provided the answer. It was procured for £200 and after many months of work, lots of expensive marine ply and the addition of an old Morris Minor car engine, he had his cruiser at last. That summer he cruised all round the Moray Firth. Life was good.

But sailing isn't always straightforward and returning from Nairn one day with his wife and mother-in-law aboard, the weather turned for the worse. With a rising wind from the north he had difficulty in reaching Balintore, the motor packed up and to make matters worse, the jib tore. David confidently decided to make a run for the Sutors, make a landfall at Nigg and phone for a lift home. His crew did not share his confidence and disappeared below to invoke help from a higher authority while clinging fervently to the mast. Through the open hatch his wife Trish spotted a large tanker steaming into the firth and demanded that her skipper ask for a tow. She was not pleased, nor was her mother, when David asserted that this was not a reasonable course of action. His boat and his marriage survived that episode and soon he was off for a cruise down the Caledonian Canal.

The inevitable happened. After locking out with a folkboat, both craft hoisted sail and beat up towards Fortrose. The folkboat sliced away with ease. David's converted lifeboat, despite her deepened and lengthened keel did not sail well to windward and never would. His boat was not his pride and joy anymore. He had to have something faster and more weatherly. Entering into partnership with A V Macleod, he bought a Halcyon 27 lying at Findhorn; long-keeled, 4 berths, galley and heads, he had a real sea boat at last. Balintore was not a suitable harbour for such a craft and so he came to Invergordon Boating Club. There, he found not only a deep water mooring for his boat, but also members who were welcoming and helpful to novices.

Until then David had never considered racing. But in the new-found spirit of camaraderie he decided to have a go. They came in last. Back in the clubhouse Duncan Murray, who had already made them very welcome, encouragingly pointed out that if David had managed to save only seven seconds he would have come second last. This proved to be possible, and then he saved another seven seconds, and eventually he won a race. So began a passion for racing which took him far beyond the confines of the Cromarty Firth to compete at Oban in West Highland Week, gaining a creditable third place and enjoying the delights of cruising that only the west coast can offer.

From such humble beginnings on a limited budget, the joys of sailing among beautiful islands to sheltered idyllic anchorages in the company of seals, whales and dolphins, the fun and excitement of racing and the fellowship of sharing a hobby with friendly and helpful enthusiasts of like mind - that is what membership of Invergordon Boating Club means to so many.

The Royal Yacht Squadron was once described as the most exclusive club in the world. That is not the nature of Invergordon Boating Club. With a welcome for everyone, regardless of experience or financial status, it can fairly claim to be one of the most inclusive clubs in the world.

Appendix 1

The Club Trophies

Mrs MacLeod of Cadboll Challenge Trophy: 26 July 1901
Invergordon Town Council Challenge Cup: 16 August 1901

Interest in the club's history had been recorded in the late 1970s and it appears some discussion took place on which was the club's first trophy. The Mrs Macleod of Cadboll Challenge Trophy Cup and the Invergordon Town Council Challenge Cup were both awarded at the first regatta in 1901. At a meeting of the Provisional Sub-Committee on 16 July 1901 before the club was officially in existence (the club was formally constituted and so came into existence at a public meeting a week later), it is minuted that the secretary had written to the Town Council asking for their support. He had not yet had a reply but read an extract from the Town Council Minutes which indicated that the councillors would be 'pleased to give their influence and patronage and would help the Boating Club in any way they could'. This is certainly the first indication of any patronage being offered to the club but the record does not determine the nature of that patronage although later evidence suggests a presumption that it would be in the form of a cup. However, the minute of the formal public meeting on 22nd July 1901, the actual birthday of the club as this was the day on which it was first constituted, shows that when the secretary was asked to name those who had agreed to give prizes only one was mentioned. Mrs MacLeod of Cadboll, wife of the first President, would present a trophy which would become the property of the winner if won three times in succession. This announcement was greeted with applause.

It is further minuted on 26th July that Mrs Macleod of Cadboll's Challenge Trophy was gratefully accepted by the club and lists the conditions for award. On 29th July the programme for the regatta was drawn up. Cash prizes were to be awarded for the first three places in each race but the first prize in the Race Open to All-comers was to be Mrs MacLeod of Cadboll's Trophy in addition to the cash prize. There is still no mention of a cup from the town council until, in a minute dated 8th August, it is recorded that the secretary 'had heard nothing from the Burgh Commissioners regarding their cup but that there was a rumour that they wished it to be given to a race for four-oared boats'. It is recorded that the Boating Club would have preferred it to be given for competition for Class A boats if this was agreeable to the donors. So, with a week left before the first regatta, the club had accepted Mrs Macleod's trophy but still had only a rumour of another from the Town Council. When the advert for the first regatta appeared in The Invergordon Times on 14th August, Mrs MacLeod's Trophy was still the only trophy listed. From this evidence it is clear that Mrs MacLeod of Cadboll's Challenge Trophy was therefore the first in the possession of Invergordon Boating Club. The Town Council Challenge Cup did however make its rumoured appearance at the regatta and was presented for racing in four-oared boats.

Club records of the early 1950s are scanty, recording only the decisions taken at the Annual General Meeting but Mrs MacLeod's Trophy is last mentioned in a press report of the Regatta in 1950 when it was awarded for competition by the converted airborne lifeboats of RAF Kinloss Yacht Club and was won by Sgt Black. In a similar event in 1951 Sgt Black competed again, this time winning what was reported to be the Invergordon Sailing Club Trophy; as no mention of a trophy with this title appears anywhere else it may have been Mrs MacLeod's Trophy which was again offered for competition by the RAF boats. Mrs MacLeod's Trophy is never mentioned again in club records.

There has been speculation that it may be the cup now known as the Nigg Cup, which is competed for annually in a race from Invergordon to Cromarty. This cup is of unknown origin and bears no inscription but it is of an ornate antique appearance although much of the silver plating has been worn through to a grey base metal. Mrs MacLeod's cup however was described as being of silver and gilt on copper and it seems unlikely that she would present a cup without having it appropriately inscribed with the donor's name. The trophy was reported in the press to be a reproduction of the Cellini Cup which was held in the

Kunsthistorisches Museum in Vienna and was the work of Benvenuto Cellini of Florence, a famous 16th century sculptor and goldsmith. An enquiry has been unable to substantiate this however. The museum asserts that the only authenticated work of Cellini in their possession is a renowned silver and gilt salt cellar.

The Littlejohn of Invercharron Challenge Cup

For many years the mistaken belief was held that this trophy had been presented to Invergordon Boating Club in 1905. It was, however, placed in the trust of the Invergordon Town Council by a Deed of Gift. This was an important safeguard for such a valuable trophy in the event of the club ceasing to exist, as happened with the onset of war in 1914.

First awarded at the regatta in 1906, it was offered for competition again at the regattas in the twenties and thirties. In 1933 a new open-air, sea-water swimming pool was opened and after the Second World War the Boating Club had no further interest in staging swimming events. Swimming was then taking place in the more civilised, if still rather chilly, environs of the swimming pool. It remained in the possession of the Town Council until the re-organisation of local government in 1975 when it was taken into the care of Ross & Cromarty District Council Leisure Services Department in Dingwall where it remained on display in an office.

With further reorganisation in 1996, the Highland Council now became the guardian of the trophy but by this time Jean Cheyne had begun researching the club's history and had laid claim to the trophy on behalf of the club. The evidence in the form of the original Deed of Gift was recovered from the Highland Council Archives and revealed that the club had no claim to ownership of the trophy, but did have rightful claim to the Trophy for any life-saving competition run by the club. However, by this time the new swimming pool had been opened in Invergordon Leisure Centre and life-saving classes were being held. It was then argued that the trophy should return to Invergordon to be presented for life-saving competition within the warmer waters of the new pool. As a result of Jean's intervention this valuable and historic trophy has been returned to the town.

This impressive cup, standing two feet high and

Dinghy Fun.

Starting Canon

Club Racing at Invergordon.

Marie Louise.
Charlie Murdoch's beautiful cruising ketch.

New Invergordon Boating Clubhouse at Rosskeen.
Opened in 1980 by Mr Ian Ross, Honorary Member.

Interior of new Clubhouse.
Centre: Isobel Bruse - a treasure of a treasurer, whose workload was formidable during the period of transfer from Invergordon to Rosskeen.

Right: David Bruce sailed the beautiful *Dragon Scylla,* and later a Hunter 19, *Chasseur,* with Isobel as crew.

Start of Season Launch.

Invergordon Boating Club's first race from the new boathouse resulted:

1. D. L. Murray, "Imagaen";
2. David Lipp, "Marella";
3. J. K. Clark, "C-Plane".

From the Ross-shire Journal, May, 1979.

weighing 83 ounces, is fashioned from solid silver and is a reproduction of an old German vase of the 16th century. Included in the gift was a six feet tall display case for the trophy, supported by legs carved with a Celtic design for Good Luck, with gold, silver and bronze medals for the leading competitors and an investment of £83 in Japanese Imperial Government stock to ensure funding for medals in future years. An engraving of a coracle such as may have been used by the inhabitants of Ross and Cromarty around 50AD has been modelled on the top, with nine lions' heads round the sides from which hang shields bearing the names of the winners; on the base are thistles and deer grass. The cup stands on a base of oak cut from a tree at Invercharron with silver plates bearing the inscription 'Invercharron House', front and back, while on either side are representations of life saving in Invergordon AD 50 and 1906. The cup, medals and Deed of Gift were displayed for a time in London before being formally received by the Town Council on Monday 13th August 1906 on behalf of the community. The Deed of Gift is beautifully illuminated and hand wrought on vellum; it is now in the safe keeping of the Highland Council Archivist. The competition rules that competitors must be clothed in shirt, trousers and shoes with a minimum weight of two and a half pounds when dry. They are required to swim 75 yards by breast stroke towards a supposed drowning person, and finish the last 25 yards carrying the victim by the first method of rescue described in the Handbook of the Royal Life-Saving Society. The competition is open to persons resident in Ross and Cromarty for at least three months prior to the competition, all ranks of the Royal Navy from ships anchored in the Cromarty Firth at the time of the competition and all ranks serving at Fort George. While the cup was to be retained for a year by the Town Council of the district in which the winner was living, the medals became the absolute property of the winners.

Lord Brassey Challenge Trophy

The Lord Brassey Challenge Trophy was presented to the club in 1904 on the first of his many visits to the Cromarty Firth with his famous yacht *Sunbeam,* an elegant three masted 170 ft steel hulled schooner built in 1874. One of the most renowned yachtsmen of the Victorian period, Thomas Brassey had applied himself as a young man to the study of navigation becoming the first yachtsman to obtain a Master's Certificate from the Board of Trade. He travelled extensively, completing a round the world voyage in 1876/77, and subsequently sailed her to the West Indies, USA, Canada, Iceland, the Mediterranean and India. He also spent many years around the turn of the century cruising the waters around Ireland and the West Coast of Scotland, noting on these trips the availability of fishermen for the reinforcement of the Royal Naval Reserve.

Born in 1836, he entered politics as MP for Hastings and was later elevated to the peerage during Gladstone's administration, becoming Civil Lord of the Admiralty. During a 5 year spell as Governor of Victoria, Australia, he visited every port in Australia and New Zealand. Ever the politician, his observations on all his cruises were reported to Parliament, his purpose always being to combine the pleasure of yachting with efforts to promote the public advantage and during the Great War *Sunbeam* served as a Hospital ship in the Mediterranean. Lord Brassey died in 1918 and *Sunbeam* was presented to the Nautical College at Pangbourne in 1919.

The Rhodesia Cup

Presented in 1904, this trophy was the gift of Invergordon born Mr H W Ross, then living in Rhodesia, and was initially awarded for competition by owners of boats living within the Cromarty Firth area.

Mr Ross was the eldest son of J C Ross and brother of D M Ross who owned a baker and confectioner's business in Invergordon on the site of what is now the newsagents near the crossroads in the centre of the town. Visited by his brother in 1909, Mr Ross had by then become Mayor of Salisbury, Rhodesia. By 1911 Alex Macandie had won the cup outright by virtue of his three victories in *Petunia* and *Little Auk*.

The Countess of Moray Challenge Trophy

Lady Moray, Dowager Countess of Moray became a patron of the club and offered this cup in October 1905; it was first offered for competition the following year. It was won outright by Alex Macandie in *Petunia* in 1913 after having won it three times.

The Walter Philip Trophy

Also known as the Russian Silver, this trophy consists of a silver tray, ladle, tankard and six goblets of Russian design and hallmark. According to the Ross-shire Journal, Mr Philip was from London and had leased Invergordon Castle for the months of August and September in 1905.

George Bankes of Balconie Challenge Trophy

Mr Bankes was a patron of the club until the 1930s and first offered this trophy for rowing in two-oared boats in August 1905.

A Wylie Hill of Lemlair Challenge Cup

Mr Wylie Hill of Lemlair donated this cup for plain keeled open boats in August 1907, the first winner being James MacLeod of Invergordon in *Fear Not*. Keen to encourage interest in sailing, he gifted his boat *La Perita* to the club in 1908. It was available for hire by members until sold in 1912 to Mr Eddie for the sum of £3.

Sir Kenneth Matheson of Lochalsh Challenge Cup

Sir Kenneth Matheson was the proprietor of Gledfield in the Parish of Kincardine on the shores of the Dornoch Firth. He inherited Ardross Castle on his father's death but much preferred his west coast home, Duncraig Castle at Plockton, and sold the Ardross Estate to Dyson Perrins in 1898. On accepting an invitation to become a patron of the club in August 1908, he offered to present a trophy for competition. The committee thanked him for his generosity but declined the offer as they claimed there was no competition for which such a cup could be offered. However, the following year a motor boat race was introduced for which there was no trophy and Sir Kenneth attended the regatta in 1909 with a party of friends to present his cup to the first winner, M Macleod of Invergordon. Motor Boat races were staged until 1933. There is no record of any in the immediate post-war period but they were resumed for a short spell in the 1960s.

Ian M Matheson of Pollo Challenge Cup

Mr Matheson donated cash prizes and this cup for the first three boats in class C, under 17 feet in length. It was handed over to the club in August 1913.

The Balblair Ferry Challenge Cup

The Balblair Ferry had a long association with the club, bringing spectators over from the Black Isle and frequently providing an unofficial rescue service to boats overturned in races. The cup was presented to the club in 1927 by Mrs Summers.

Roderick Robertson Challenge Cup

Miss Helen Edwina Robertson of Chicago USA, a patron of the club, presented this cup in 1928. Roderick Robertson of Chicago USA was also a Patron of the club.

The Commodore's Cup and Flag

Mr William Martineau became the club's first Commodore in 1931. Though not an active sailor himself, he had been a patron and vice-president of the club since its reformation in 1925 and, on accepting the position of Commodore, he offered a magnificent cup and a flag to be flown for the season by the winning boat. His tenure of office was, however, shortlived as a result of the club's demise in 1933. Awarded a knighthood in 1935 for his political and social achievement, Sir William's family were descended from the Huguenots, French Protestants in the 16th and 17th century, who were forced to leave the country and settled in England. Heir on the female side of the MacKenzies of Redcastle and Kincraig, he inherited the Kincraig Estate on his mother's death in 1916, improving the farm steadings of Kincraig, Tomich and Invergordon Mains. He acquired Invergordon Castle from a Larbert Timber Merchant who had bought it from MacLeod of Cadboll in 1919; being in a state of disrepair and having suffered the ravages of fire, it was demolished in 1928. Stone from the castle was reputedly used to build The House of Rosskeen, occupied by his son Captain Roderick MacKenzie of the Seaforth Highlanders and later Major HAC MacKenzie of Dalmore, another active Boating Club member in the post-war years.

Sir William contributed several trophies to local sporting organisations and was also Chieftain of Invergordon Highland Gathering. He died in 1950 aged 84 and Kincraig estate was finally sold in 1964. Kincraig House is now a hotel.

The Duke of Sutherland Cup

The 4th Duke of Sutherland, one of the club's early patrons and a member of the Royal Yacht Squadron at Cowes, offered a cup for competition in October

1905. *Elf* having won it in three successive years 1926, 1927 and 1928 won this cup outright. His son, who had succeeded to the title in 1913, was then approached and asked to consider donating a replacement for the trophy given by his father but he declined to do so.

The Dalmore Cup

Following the Duke of Sutherland's disinclination to donate another cup, Major W F MacKenzie of Dalmore then offered The Dalmore Cup for competition by A Class centreboard boats. His offer was accepted by the club on 19 April 1932.

Major MacKenzie had been a keen competitor in the early years of the club's existence; his father Major A MacKenzie had been a founder member and one of the club's first vice-presidents and his son, Col HAC MacKenzie was a keen racer and cruiser in the post war period until the late 1970s. In the fourth generation of this family, Lieutenant Roderick MacKenzie of the Queen's Own Highlanders was honoured by the Royal Cruising Club of Great Britain with their 1984 award for Bravery and Seamanship following his action in assisting a yacht in distress in the Mediterranean

Sea the previous summer. His brother James was tragically drowned in January 1984 when his car slid off an icy Belleport pier only a few yards from the clubhouse as he was checking the family boat during stormy weather.

The 1932 Challenge Trophy

The matter of weekly races had been the subject of some discussion and in 1932 rules for a weekly series of races were drawn up. Breaking with tradition, it appears that the club purchased this trophy as no donor has been mentioned in the minutes. The cup was awarded to the winner of the series of five races and was presented on the night of the regatta.

MacKay Cup

The structural engineering company W H MacKay of Fearn presented this cup for competition by Class B boats in the Moray Firth Cruiser Race in 1983.

The Keel Wheel Trophy

This is the one no one wants to win. It is presented to the skipper who has achieved the dubious distinction of having had the most spectacular grounding of the season. Introduced by Liz Fraser as a surprise at an annual dinner dance and presentation of prizes during her spell as Commodore, it consists of a piece of driftwood on casters, symbolic of a device to ease under the keel to run the boat off on wheels with a brass plate inscribed with the names of the winners. Martin Ryan, a very skillful sailor but one whose competitiveness drives him to take risks, has logged most wins to date and is the current holder. The holder has the honour of nominating the winner for the following year.

Invergordon Distillers Bowl

A silver quaich was presented to the Aquatic Club in 1963 by the distillery at Invergordon.
Following the amalgamation with Invergordon Sailing Club in 1965 this cup with the two following trophies became the property of the re-formed Invergordon Boating Club.

Caledonian Cup

Also thought to have been presented to the Aquatic club, the donor of this cup may have been the Caledonian Bar, as many a happy hour was spent there after sailing.

The Leslie Trophy

Presented to the Invergordon Aquatic Club in 1963 by Mr and Mrs Leslie who had a hairdressing business in the town. Mrs Leslie was the daughter of Provost Walter H George of Invergordon.

The following two swimming trophies are still in the club's possession and have now been offered to Invergordon Swimming Pool for annual competition but they will remain in the ownership of Invergordon Boating Club.

The Honourable Hugh D McIntosh Cup

The Hon Hugh D McIntosh M.L.C. a renowned Australian business man, presented this impressive trophy for the ladies' swimming competitions held at the regattas in the inter-war years. It was first presented in 1927. A handsome trophy with decorative feathering around the base it bears a coat of arms with the motto Arma Pacis Fulcra. No inscriptions were allowed on this trophy and medals were awarded to the winner.

Commander Roper RN Challenge Cup

Commander Roper of *HMS Chameleon* presented this trophy for the Boy Scouts' swimming race at the annual regatta in 1913. It was first won by Scout Stuart of Fortrose.

Appendix 2

INVERGORDON BOATING CLUB
PRESIDENTS AND COMMODORES

1901-1914 Capt R W MacLeod of Cadboll
1925-1926 Maj Mackenzie of Dalmore
1926-1929 Baillie J E MacDonald
1929-1930 Ex-Baillie J E MacDonald
1930-1931 Mr D Marshall

First Commodore
1931-1933 William Martineau of Kincraig

- - - - - - - - - - - - - -

1948-1950 Hugh Ross
1950-1955 Cdr J R Westmacott
1959-1963 No records
1963-1964 Hugh Ross

- - - - - - - - - - - - - -

Amalgamation with Aquatic Club
1965-1966 Cdr Elwin
1966-1968 John Burgess
1968-1972 Iain Ross

1972-1974 Douglas L Young
1974-1975 H Clement
1975-1976 Douglas L Young
1976-1978 Duncan L Murray
1978-1980 Donald Stevenson
1980-1982 Douglas L Young
1982-1985 Ronald Stewart
1985-   Duncan L Murray
1985-1986 Charles Murdoch (Temp)
            (Vice Commodore)
1986-1987 Alastair Bulman
1987-1988 Henry Westphal
1988-1991 Charles Murdoch
1991-1993 Martin Ryan
1993-1996 Liz Fraser
1996-1999 Donald McDonald
1999-   Ronald Christie

Appendix 3

INVERGORDON BOATING CLUB
HONORARY SECRETARIES

1901-1907	Major Ian Forsyth of Balintraid
1907-1911	John Brown
1911-1914	John Fraser

- - - - - - - - - - - - -

1925-1931	William George
1931-1932	Thomas Mackay
1932-1933	F F Mackay & assistant
	Duncan Chisholm

- - - - - - - - - - - - -

1948-1949	F B Carter
1949-1950	Ian Moodie
1950-1952	F B Carter
1952-1957	Philip E Durham
1957-1959	M Mackay
1959-1963	No records
1963-1964	James M Hendry

- - - - - - - - - - - - -

Amalgamation with Aquatic Club

1965-1966	Murdo MacLennan
1966-1968	Miss I McBain
1968-1971	Martin Legge
1971-1972	D Mitchell
1972-1974	John Clark
1974-1975	Douglas L Young
1975-1976	R Mitchell
1976-1978	William Bauld
1978-1980	Duncan L Murray
1980-1981	Henry Westphal
1981-	Allan MacDonald
1981-1982	Agnes Dillon (Temp)
1982-1986	Jean W Cheyne
1986-1989	Duncan L Murray
1989-1990	Ronald Stewart
1990-1998	George O'Hara
1998-	Peter D Cheyne

Appendix 3 (Cont)

INVERGORDON BOATING CLUB
HONORARY TREASURERS

1901-1914	John Robertson
1925-1930	H Paterson
1930-1931	G N I Mackay

- - - - - - - - - - - - - -

1948-1949	N Mackay
1949-1950	Mr Murchison
1950-1951	G N I Mackay
1951-1959	N Mackay
1959-1963	No records
1963-1964	James M Hendry

- - - - - - - - - - - - - -

Amalgamation with Aquatic Club

1965-1966	Miss S McIntosh
1966-1967	Mrs S Christie
1967-	Vacant
1968-1972	Ross Mitchell
1972-1973	C Simms
1973-1974	David Lipp

1974-1975	E Hay
1975-1981	Isobel Bruce
1981-1984	Agnes Dillon
1984-1987	Alastair B Bulman
1987-1988	Henry Westphal
1988-	Fred Fraser

Appendix 4

INVERGORDON BOATING CLUB SAILING SECRETARIES

The first mention of a Race Committee appears in the minute of the Annual General Meeting of 19 October 1969, namely;

D L Young : M Gowering : J Burgess

- - - - - - - - - - - - -

The first mention of the appointment of a Sailing Secretary appears in 1978.

1978-1980	Duncan L Murray
1980-	Donald Stevenson - Acting
1980-1981	Duncan L Murray
1981-1982	Vacant
1982-1983	John Dillon
1983-1984	Duncan L Murray
1984-1986	George H Shields
1986-1991	Andrew J Murray
1991-	George H Shields

INVERGORDON BOATING CLUB COMMITTEE MEMBERS 2001

Commodore:	Ronald Christie
Vice Commodore:	Donald Mackenzie
Rear Commodore:	Donald McDonald
Hon Secretary:	Peter D Cheyne
Hon Treasurer:	Frederick Fraser

- - - - - - - - - - - - -

Committee Members
David Tullis Martyn Crawshaw
Lennie Mackay Dr Jerry Jackson Gerald Landale

- - - - - - - - - - - - -

Sailing Secretary: George Shields
Sailing Committee: Flag Officers and
Martyn Ryan   Terry MacLeod
George O'Hara   Neil Cormack

- - - - - - - - - - - - -

Beachmaster: Ronald Stewart